MW01061809

CAN A CATHOLIC BE A SOCIALIST?

[THE ANSWER IS NO-HERE'S WHY]

TRENT HORN & CATHERINE R. PAKALUK

Catholic Answers Press

© 2020 Trent Horn and Catherine R. Pakaluk

All rights reserved. Except for quotations, no part of this book may be reproduced or transmitted in any form or by any means, electronic or mechanical, including photocopying, recording, uploading to the internet, or by any information storage and retrieval system without written permission from the publisher.

All emphasis in Scripture citations added.

Published by Catholic Answers, Inc.
2020 Gillespie Way
El Cajon, California 92020
1-888-291-8000 orders
619-387-0042 fax
catholic.com

Printed in the United States of America

Cover and interior design by Russell Graphic Design

978-1-68357-162-9
978-1-68357-163-6 Kindle
978-1-68357-164-3 ePub

TABLE OF CONTENTS

INTRODUCTION

PART FIVE: SOCIALISM RECONSTRUCTED

APPENDIX: WHAT ABOUT DISTRIBUTISM?

ENDNOTES

ABOUT THE AUTHORS

INTRODUCTION

In the middle of the third century, the Roman emperor Valerian launched a fierce persecution against the Church that resulted in the martyrdom of Pope Saint Sixtus II along with seven deacons. St. Ambrose tells us that when the Roman authorities demanded that one of the deacons, named Lawrence, hand over "the treasures of the Church," he agreed. According to Ambrose, "On the following day he brought the poor together. When asked where the treasures were which he had promised, he pointed to the poor, saying, "These are the treasures of the Church."

Christ commanded his followers to care for the poor and warned them that ignoring the poor was the same as ignoring *him* (Matt 25:40). As the Church grew within the Roman Empire, Christians became famous for their generosity, which included not just almsgiving but the construction of the first hospitals that served the poor. The Roman emperor Julian the Apostate lamented how Christians "support not only their own poor but ours as well; all men see that our people lack aid from us." For the most marginalized people in Roman society, like widows and abandoned newborns, it was only the generosity of Christians that stood between them and a premature death.

Christian generosity continued to be the difference between life and death for many people even after Christians became the rulers of medieval kingdoms, in which there simply wasn't enough wealth for the state to lift the masses out of poverty. But this began to change with the rise of modern capitalism, as is evident in Adam Smith's famous 1776 essay, "An Inquiry into the Nature and Causes of the Wealth of Nations." Christians now had the ability to *create* wealth, and with that power came moral questions about how to address the perennial problem of poverty.

In the century after Smith's essay was published, revolutionaries in America and Europe tore down the authority of the monarchy and replaced it with democratic republics. Ultimate authority, the revolutionaries said, should lie with the people instead of the king. Other revolutionaries took this democratic ideal even further and said wealth and property should not lie with a few people (be they monarchs or capitalists) but should be owned by all. In 1871, some of these revolutionaries even took over the city of Paris for two months, establishing a "socialist commune" until the French army retook the city, killing thousands of *communards* in the process.

By the end of the nineteenth century, the revolutionary spirit showed no sign of slowing and even many Christians were becoming sympathetic to the socialist cause. Christians now had access to more wealth and political power than they had ever possessed in the history of the world, but it wasn't clear how those things should be used to help the poor. All of this was on the mind of Pope Leo XIII as he wrote the introduction to the most famous papal encyclical to address the issue of socialism: *Rerum Novarum* (Latin: "New Things"). He says this "spirit of revolutionary change" is not surprising and notes:

> The elements of the conflict now raging are unmistakable, in the vast expansion of industrial pursuits and the marvelous discoveries of science; in the changed relations between masters and workmen; in the enormous fortunes of some few individuals, and the utter poverty of the masses; the increased self-reliance and closer mutual combination of the working classes; as also, finally, in the prevailing moral degeneracy.

The pope goes on to describe how everyone is talking about these "new things" and so the Church, which teaches us on matters of faith and morals, "thought it expedient now to speak on the condition of the working classes."

The socialist revolutions of the nineteenth century spurred the creation of the Church's *social doctrine*: the application of its teaching to issues that arise as society changes over time. When it comes to the application of timeless truths to changing circumstances the pope admitted:

> The discussion is not easy, nor is it void of danger. It is no easy matter to define the relative rights and mutual duties of the rich and of the poor, of capital and of labor. And the danger lies in this, that crafty agitators are intent on making use of these differences of opinion to pervert men's judgments and to stir up the people to revolt.

Although much has changed in the century since Pope Leo XIII penned these words, many things are still the same. There may not today be calls for violent revolution in America or Europe, but there are grassroots movements seeking to establish socialism through democratic activism. Some of those movements even claim that a Christian is obligated to support socialist economies or else he does not truly follow Christ's command to "love your neighbor as yourself."

In this book we will apply the Church's social doctrine to the debate on socialism and show that not only are Catholics not obligated to be socialists, they—we—*cannot* be socialists. It is not a permissible or prudent way to address the problem of poverty.

In part one, we will examine the modern resurgence of socialism and explain why so many people, including faithful Catholics, are attracted to this ideology. Then we will "pull back the curtain" and show why socialism is an inherently contradictory and unsustainable approach to economics.

In part two we will refute the claim that Christianity gave birth to socialism and show how it was actually conceived in nineteenth-century Europe. We'll also explore Pope Leo XIII's arguments against socialism, especially his claim that it violates the natural right to private property and poses a grave danger to the family.

In part three we continue our historical survey and reveal, in all its horrors, the destruction socialism wrought in the twentieth century.

In part four we turn our attention to capitalism and, while not providing an exhaustive summary and defense, refute arguments that try to justify socialism by saying capitalism is worse or unacceptable as an economic system.

Finally, in part five, we return to the present to examine modern, Catholic defenses of socialism and present a trajectory toward a "moral capitalism." For the best approach to economics will not only produce the most wealth and alleviate the most poverty, but will create conditions for the human spirit to flourish, grow in virtue, and be perfected by God's grace.

PART ONE

SOCIALISM DECONSTRUCTED

1
THE RETURN OF SOCIALISM

In 2019, 43 percent of Americans consider socialism to be a "good thing" and millennials are some of its strongest supporters.[1] Magazines such as *Teen Vogue* even run articles like "Everything You Should Know About Karl Marx" and "What 'Capitalism' Is and How It Affects People," which says that millennials "expect a grand societal shift toward socialism" to counteract a "dystopian Mad Max nightmare" in which "rich plutocrats own everything." Another poll found that half of young people say they would prefer life in a socialist country to a capitalist one.[2]

But this flirtation with socialism is nothing new; in order to understand it, in fact, we need to go back to the Great Depression. When you see how socialism thrived in that decade, you'll understand why it's making such a comeback today.

SHARE THE WEALTH

By the mid-1930s, following the stock market crash in 1929, the average family's income had fallen 40 percent. But maybe they were the lucky ones compared to the 25 percent of Americans who were unemployed.[3] For many people, volatile markets and greedy bankers were the villains responsible for taking people's jobs and even their homes. In John Steinbeck's 1939 novel *The Grapes of Wrath,* banks are described as "monsters" that men make but can't control, and capitalists are depicted as heartless pursuers of profit. For example, in one scene Steinbeck describes farmers dousing oranges in kerosene as starving people look on, because this was necessary to keep the price of oranges from getting too low.

Steinbeck doesn't tell his readers that it was the federal government that ordered the farmers to do this. However, he does describe the resentment many average people felt toward an economy that seemed to benefit the rich at the expense of the poor: "Men who have created new fruits in the world cannot create a system whereby their fruits may be eaten . . . in the eyes of the hungry there is a growing wrath. In the souls of the people the grapes of wrath are filling and growing heavy, growing heavy for the vintage."[4]

Before 1929, the Communist Party USA was a marginal movement, but during the thirties its explosive growth in membership led later historians to call that decade "the heyday of American Communism."[5] However, most critics of capitalism adopted a more moderate socialism focused on redistributing wealth instead of launching a worker's revolution. For example, Democratic senator Huey Long blamed the country's economic crisis on the small number of people who he said owned most of the nation's wealth. In his notorious "Share Our Wealth Speech," Long declared:

[T]he rich people of this country—and by rich people I mean the super-rich—will not allow us to solve the problems, or rather the one little problem that is afflicting this country, because in order to cure all of our woes it is necessary to scale down the big fortunes, that we may scatter the wealth to be shared by all of the people.[6]

Long proposed that no one be allowed to possess more than $50 million. He claimed that confiscatory taxation on wealth above that amount could provide every family with enough money to own a home, automobile, and radio, meaning that "there will be no such thing as a family living in poverty and distress."

Despite such lofty promises, socialism didn't catch on in America, partly because it was associated with distinctly anti-American values. While reflecting on his unsuccessful 1936 bid for the California governorship, socialist Upton Sinclair said, "The American people will take socialism, but they won't take the label. . . . Running on the Socialist ticket I got 60,000 votes, and running on the slogan to 'End Poverty in California' I got 879,000."[7]

HISTORY REPEATS ITSELF

In the 2010s, struggling American families were still reeling from the Great Recession, after which the average family's income fell by 4 percent and nine million jobs were lost—doubling the unemployment rate to a high of 9.3 percent.[8] What angered people the most, however, were policies that seemed to allow the wealthy to hoard the country's wealth at the expense of the poor. In 2011, protesters took over lower Manhattan as part of the "Occupy Wall Street" movement, carrying signs saying, "We are the 99 percent."

That slogan came from economist Joseph Stiglitz's article "Of the 1 percent, by the 1 percent, for the 1 percent," in which Stiglitz claimed that 1 percent of the population controlled 40 percent of the nation's wealth and that, although their incomes had risen over the past twenty-five years, the incomes of the lower classes were stagnant or had even fallen. He ominously concluded:

> The top 1 percent have the best houses, the best educations, the best doctors, and the best lifestyles, but there

is one thing that money doesn't seem to have bought: an understanding that their fate is bound up with how the other 99 percent live. Throughout history, this is something that the top 1 percent eventually do learn. Too late.[9]

Part of young people's affection for socialism is grounded in a distrust of capitalism that grew out of the Great Recession. Many millennials blamed the economic crisis on unregulated free markets, and polls show that between 2010 and 2018 their support for capitalism dropped from 68 percent to 45 percent.[10] This skepticism made them the least likely generation in history to invest their savings for retirement. Some of them even believe retirement saving is pointless because, as one thirty-two-year-old political consultant put it, "I don't think the world can sustain capitalism for another decade. It's socialism or bust."[11]

Some of the most vocal advocates for socialism, though, are Christian theologians and committed Catholics. The Tradinista! Movement identifies itself as "a small party of young Christian socialists committed to traditional orthodoxy, to a politics of virtue and the common good, and to the destruction of capitalism, and its replacement by a truly social political economy."[12] In 2019, Eastern Orthodox theologian David Bentley Hart published an editorial in the *New York Times* with the provocative title, "Can We Please Relax About Socialism?"[13] Not to be outdone, the Jesuit magazine *America* published a feature-length article later that year entitled, "The Catholic Case for Communism."[14]

There's no small irony in this new enthusiasm for socialism among young Christians, when you consider that socialism served as the "founding heresy" that spurred the development of Catholic social teaching.

Between the 1840s and the 1940s, the papacy released eight major encyclicals that dealt with the subject, all in critical ways. In 1849, Pope Pius IX referred to "the wicked theories of this socialism and Communism" and how they plotted to "overthrow the entire order of human affairs" through the haze of "perverted teachings" (*Nostis et Nobiscum* 6). At the end of the nineteenth century, Pope Leo XIII called socialism a "deadly plague" (*Quod Apostolici Muneris* 1) that reaps a "harvest of misery" (*Graves de Communi Re* 21). Thirty years later, Pope Pius XI said, "Communism is intrinsically wrong, and no one who would save Christian civilization may collaborate with it in any undertaking whatsoever" (*Divini Redemptoris* 58).

"REAL" SOCIALISTS

Many socialists, when confronted with the moral and economic failures of countries like the Soviet Union, are quick to respond, "Oh no, I don't want *that* kind of socialism" or, "That wasn't *real* socialism, that was Communism." They don't want a totalitarian government that controls everyone; they just want a benevolent government that helps everyone. In polling, this leads to a mixed bag of preferences.

For example, two-thirds of millennials support free college tuition, government-provided universal health care, and a government guarantee of food, shelter, and a living wage. But the majority of them also oppose state ownership of private businesses and tax increases on anyone but the wealthy.[15] Another survey shows that whereas only 56 percent of people have a positive image of "capitalism," 86 percent have a positive image of "entrepreneurs."[16] One *Atlantic* writer ably summarizes this paradoxical attitude toward economics: "They'd like Washington to fix everything, just so long as it doesn't run anything."[17] Hart evinces a similar attitude when he claims of the United States:

Only here is the word "socialism" freighted with so much perceived menace. I take this to be a symptom of our unique national genius for stupidity. In every other free society with a functioning market economy, socialism is an ordinary, rather general term for sane and compassionate governance of the public purse for the purpose of promoting general welfare and a more widespread share in national prosperity.[18]

So who's right? Is socialism a deadly plague that reaps a harvest of misery? Or is it a sane and compassionate economic policy that everyone, especially Christians, should support?

There are a lot of things that are wrong in Hart's op-ed, but he does make one good point. He writes, "In this country we employ terms like 'socialism' with wanton indifference to historical details and conceptual distinctions." Indeed, critics who cry wolf and describe every form of governmental economic intervention as "socialism" numb people to the unique evils that occur in a truly socialist system.

That's why in order to determine if Catholics can be socialists we have to first understand "real socialism."

IT'S IMPORTANT TO REMEMBER . . .

- Socialism often becomes popular during times of economic turmoil.
- Most people have an incoherent understanding of socialism and often conflate it with government entitlement programs.

- The Catholic Church has consistently and strongly denounced socialism as an evil that Christians can never support.

2
WHAT IS SOCIALISM?

When most people think of the "Pilgrims," they think of people in big hats eating luxurious Thanksgiving feasts. But in the spring of 1621, the Plymouth colonists were in danger of starving to death and, despite what you were told in elementary school, it wasn't harsh weather or ignorance about farming that led to these dire circumstances. Instead, it was the pilgrims' policy of sharing communal plots of land that nearly led to their ruin.

Even after local tribes helped the pilgrims survive their first harsh winter, the colonists still suffered from food shortages. That was because people weren't allowed to grow their own food. Instead, food was grown communally and then equally distributed to everyone—even to people who didn't help farm any of it. In choosing this method of farming, the colony's governor William Bradford said the pilgrims thought "the taking away of property, and bringing in community into a commonwealth, would make them happy and flourishing; as if they were wiser than God."[19]

It took several painful years for the pilgrims to learn they were not so wise.

THAT WHICH IS COMMON

According to Bradford's journal, the strongest of the young men complained about "spend[ing] their time and strength to work for other men's wives and children without any recompense." Wives viewed forced work for other husbands and families as "a kind of slavery." Even the older residents who couldn't work (and thus actually had more to eat than they otherwise would have) "thought it some indignity and disrespect unto them."

People were mad because no matter how hard they worked, their situation in life wouldn't improve. And they resented neighbors who barely worked but still got the same rations as they did. These bitter colonists may have thought, "I'm done with back-breaking work in the fields. Instead, I'll just do the bare minimum like everybody else."

The communal farming system could tolerate a few lazy people as long as everyone else worked hard. But once enough people only had incentive to do the bare minimum, then it would only take bad luck or uncooperative weather to ruin their meager food supplies. Fortunately, Bradford recognized that because "all men have this corruption in them, God in his wisdom saw another course fitter for them."

He responded to the crisis by assigning each family its own parcel of land and letting them keep the food they produced. Bradford recalled, "This had very good success; for it made all hands very industrious, so as much more corn was planted than otherwise would have been." Bradford had discovered what the Greek philosopher Aristotle proved to be true 2,500 years ago: "That which is common to the greatest number has the least care bestowed upon it. Everyone thinks chiefly of his own, hardly at all of the common interest." He added that a person only thinks of the common good "when he is himself concerned as an individual."[20]

The sad truth is that every generation has individuals in it who fail to learn this lesson about human nature. The pilgrim's plight isn't just interesting history; it's a cautionary tale that shows why no one (especially Catholics who share the pilgrim's worship of "God in his wisdom") should be a socialist.

THE MEANING OF SOCIALISM

One May 2019 poll revealed that a third of people associate socialism with providing people with health care, housing, and jobs, and ending poverty, while 20 percent don't know what socialism is. Only one in five could name the mechanisms by which socialism is supposed to achieve its grand promises: government ownership of the economy and the abolishment of private property.[21]

Bhaskar Sunkara, editor of the popular socialist magazine *Jacobin,* writes, "Radically changing things would mean taking away the source of capitalists' power: the private ownership of property."[22] Sunkara faithfully adheres to the teachings of the most famous socialist in history, Karl Marx, who declared in *The Communist Manifesto* that "the theory of the Communists may be summed up in the single sentence: abolition of private property."[23] This is why Pope Leo XIII said socialism is contrary to the natural right to own property and that, "the main tenet of socialism, [the] community of goods, must be utterly rejected" (*Rerum Novarum* 15).

This communal ownership of wealth and property also means that no one could *exchange* privately owned goods in order to make a profit. Instead, society would simply produce goods by the command of government-owned industries, and those industries alone would sell them. Political scientist Frances Fox Piven notes, "The academic debates about socialism's 'meaning' are huge and arcane and rife with disagreements, but what all definitions have in common is either the elimination of the market or its strict containment."[24]

Such regimes are called *command economies* or *planned economies* because in order for such a system to work without a market (a means for people to voluntarily buy and sell from one another) the economy would have to be centrally planned. Administrators and bureaucrats—accountants, economists, and statisticians—would have to direct factories, farms, and businesses (or what are commonly grouped under the term "the means of production") to produce enough of the right kind of goods and services that people desire, or at the very least, need.

In his book *Socialism . . . Seriously: A Brief Guide to Human Liberation*, activist Danny Katch envisions a future in which the community produces so many goods and services that most people only have to work Tuesday through Thursday. His fictional socialist wistfully explains, "Each year the whole money thing feels increasingly pointless in a society in which everyone has more than enough of what they need and plenty of what they want. But money is still the main way for planning committees to keep track of how goods and services are being distributed and used."[25]

SOCIALISM OR COMMUNISM?

Later we will look at how central planning led to horrifying results in socialist countries like the Soviet Union, but some people may say we shouldn't use Communism's failures as an argument against socialism. After all, they say, "Communism isn't the same thing as socialism."

But according to the textbook *Essentials of Sociology* "The terms socialism and Communism are often used more or less interchangeably."[26]

For many collectivists, socialism and Communism are not separate systems of economic thought; they are successive stages in the same scheme to create a world of collective ownership. Vladimir Lenin wrote in *The State and Revolution* that, "in the first phase of communist society (usually called socialism) 'bourgeois law' is not abolished in its entirety, but only in part, only in proportion to the economic revolution so far attained."

Communism isn't the embarrassing, authoritarian cousin that gives socialism a bad name. Instead, Communism is the end point to which socialism inevitably tends, at least for Marxists.

Marx defended a limited "dictatorship of the proletariat" that would rule until a classless, Communist society came into existence. But, as we will see later, socialism has inherent authoritarian tendencies. That's why it's no surprise that any "dictatorship of the proletariat" would refuse (like almost every other dictator in history) to give up its power once its goal of creating a centrally planned economy had been achieved.

One reason Marxists give for why no socialist country has ever reached the endgame of peaceful Communism is that socialism isn't just for nations; it's for the *entire world*. Marx wanted to "abolish countries and nationality" because "the working men have no country."[27] His collaborator Friedrich Engels said that social classes "fall as inevitably as they once arose. The state inevitably falls with them." He believed the idea of a governing state belonged in "the museum of antiquities, next to the spinning wheel and the bronze axe."[28]

Modern socialists tend to follow Marx on this point, as is evident in the World Socialist Party's claim that "central to the meaning of socialism is common ownership. This means the resources of the world being owned in common by the entire global population."[29]

But not all socialists historically have wanted to adapt this "international Communism." Some preferred a "national socialism" grounded in a powerful authoritarian state. The most famous example of this approach was the German National Socialist Workers' Party, or as you probably know them, the Nazis.

The Nazi party platform required the nationalization of industries and charged the state with providing for people's livelihoods. Its defenders taught the importance of respecting the maxim, "The common good goes before the individual's good."[30] Even historians who dispute Hitler's socialist credentials admit that Nazi Germany used planning methods similar to those of socialists. According to one such historian, Ian Kershaw, this meant that "the state, not the market, would determine the shape of [Germany's] economic development."[31]

SOCIALISM OR CAPITALISM?

Another misconception about socialism is that there are only two kinds of economic systems: complete government control of the economy and complete lack of government control (so-called *laissez-faire* capitalism). But it's incorrect even to think about economic systems as existing on a control or regulatory spectrum. What divides socialism from capitalism is not whether the government controls the economy or how much it does, or how big it is, but its *role* in creating and sustaining the economy

Under socialism, governments create and sustain *the production of goods and services* by running businesses and employing individuals. In contrast, under capitalism, governments create and sustain *the conditions* under which individuals and firms produce goods and services. In a modern market economy, these conditions include a robust system of property rights that allow for the sale and transfer of property as well as regulations that set the "rules of the game" for all types of market transactions.

Many of the "freest" economies, then, actually operate under many government regulations; in fact, they couldn't exist without governments to enforce contracts that regulate all their economic exchanges.

If economies exist on a spectrum, then it isn't a spectrum of control or regulation. Instead, it's a spectrum of how many functions the central government takes to be its own, and how many are left to subsidiaries—private individuals and firms, communities, and local governments. In this book we are concerned with economies that lie toward the socialist end of that spectrum, or ones where the greater number of functions are tasked to the central government.

In this book, then, we use the terms *socialism* and *Communism* to refer to the same kind of centrally planned economic system that rejects the ownership of private property. We will show that Catholics cannot support these economic systems because they violate our natural rights and lead to human misery. Even apart from the authoritarian abuses that often accompany these systems, socialism contains undeniable flaws that make it unfit for any modern nation to accept.

IT'S IMPORTANT TO REMEMBER . . .

- Socialism is opposed to the private ownership of property and believes that the community as a whole should "own" the means of producing goods and services.

- Socialism and Communism represent different stages in the ultimate goal of eliminating economic and social classes; both systems advocate for centrally planned economies that leave no room for a free market.

- The choice in the modern world is not between socialism and completely unregulated capitalism but between keeping the means of production primarily in the hands of private businesses or primarily in the hands of government.

3
SOCIALISM'S FATAL FLAWS

If there's one thing socialists are great at doing, it's coming up with appealing visions of what a socialist future would look like. This kind of literature was especially popular in the early nineteenth century, before the gritty reality of socialism became a historical fact. One of the most popular was Étienne Cabet's 1842 novel *Voyage to Icaria*, about a traveler who visits the fictional nation of Icaria and is impressed by its cleanliness and lack of poverty.

The traveler credits this paradise to the community's abandonment of private property and its commitment to living a simple, communal lifestyle. He utters what could be considered a mantra for socialists: "Nothing is impossible for a government that wants the good of its citizens."[32] But history has repeatedly shown, in lessons that become more painful every time they must be taught, that a utopia (a word that literally means "no place") is impossible to create in this world.[33]

In fact, when we stop to think about how a socialist society would even work—beyond the presumption of "free" housing and health care for all—we see that true socialism, the kind endorsed by thinkers like Marx, aren't even hypothetical—they are impossible.

THE INCENTIVE PROBLEM

The ultimate goal of socialists, especially those influenced by Karl Marx, is the elimination of social classes. According to them, *inequalities* are the source of all conflict between human beings and so, once classes like rich and poor are a thing of the past, then conflict between human beings will cease as well. But this theory only works if "classes" aren't just noticeable differences between groups of human beings that will *always* exist.

For example, if no one were richer than anyone else because everyone received the same wages, why would anyone be motivated to choose a dirty or dangerous occupation? If you would get paid the same amount of money, would you rather make sausage or snow cones? Would you rather clean car windshields or the windows on a skyscraper?

Of course, most people will want the more pleasant job, which means that the less-desirable jobs will have to pay more. Unequal wages thus adjust compensation to *create incentives* for people to do the jobs that need to be done. But when higher wages are given according to the job, some people will naturally make more money and so Marx's dreaded "classes" will still persist.

If such incentives were abolished by giving everyone the same wages, then the less-desirable jobs will go unfilled. Or, what is more likely to happen in a command economy, some people will be *forced* to work at these jobs even against their will. Yet even then, classes will still exist—in the form of the pleasantness or safety of one's work or just its basic desirability—creating inequality and envy.

Some jobs, like oil drilling or cattle farming, require people to live in harsh climates while other jobs, like lifeguarding, let people live near the beach. Which lifestyle do you think most people would prefer? So you would be stuck with a higher class of people lucky enough to draw work assignments in Malibu and a lower class that gets stuck in Timbuktu.[34]

And you can be sure that those who have connections with governmental planners will be able to secure the pleasant upper-class jobs while the lower classes are compelled to do everyone else's dirty work.

Maybe this inequality could be solved by having people share and rotate jobs—like being a kindergarten teacher one week and a sewer repairman the next? This would only result in a society of unskilled workers, since it takes years of experience to master a trade. Yet this seems to be the solution Marx has in mind when he dreams about how, once production results in a superabundance of goods, it will be "possible for me to do one thing today and another tomorrow, to hunt in the morning, fish in the afternoon, rear cattle in the evening, criticize after dinner, just as I have a mind, without ever becoming hunter, fisherman, herdsman, or critic."[35]

Whatever conception of genteel living Marx had in mind, most of us don't want our doctor, lawyer, plumber, or electrician to be someone who was a window-washer last week, or who decided to try this field out as a hobby. Differences in wages play a huge role in getting the right people—those who have the interest, talent, or taste, to invest the right resources (e.g., specialized schooling or apprenticeship) in order do the right work—the thing that needs doing.

The incentive problem also beguiles moderate socialism, which doesn't rely on outright government control of businesses but simply confiscates wealth or income above a certain amount. If a person has no hope of retaining income above a certain amount, then he has no incentive to put in the necessary work to produce the income he never receives (and then it's the pilgrims' starvation problem all over again).

But, the biggest incentive problem for socialism lies in getting people to work in the first place.

As we shall see, socialists often complain about the injustice of having to "sell your labor-power to capitalists" in order to survive. They think that if a person's livelihood depends on how much he works, then he is just a "wage slave." They say that a socialist economy will guarantee everyone's basic needs and so no one has to be subjected to "wage slavery." But if that's true, why would anyone choose to work at all? Sure, some people may work here and there when they feel bored, but why would most people work full-time to produce the goods that other people need to live when they can get what they need without working?

Some socialists try to evade this problem with the motto, "Those who don't work, don't eat" and say they will deny freeloaders access to the community's resources (St. Paul gave this same advice in 2 Thessalonians 3:10 in order to deal with freeloaders in the early Church). But now the injustice of "selling your labor-power to capitalists" has simply been replaced with the privilege of "selling your labor-power to the state"—which, unlike businesses in a free market, doesn't have to compete for it. Even if socialists reached their "post-state" communist utopia, there would still be a class of workers in constant conflict with a class of moochers trying to game the system.

THE KNOWLEDGE PROBLEM

If you have ever watched a flock of starlings, sometimes thousands of birds, move in unison, then you know it's a mesmerizing experience. How do they all know to change direction together so quickly? It's not like there is one bird directing their movement like how a conductor directs an orchestra. Instead, each individual bird receives a cue from the birds around him and this sends an "information wave" through the whole flock letting them know which way they should go.

The knowledge of how the flock should move is dispersed among many birds. It isn't in the hands of a single bird leader who directs everything, nor could it be. And the same is true when it comes to the most important economic knowledge: the "knowledge of the particular circumstances of time and place" as 1974 economic Nobel Prize winner Friedrich Hayek called it.

"We need to remember," he said, "how much we have to learn in any occupation after we have completed our theoretical training, how big a part of our working life we spend learning particular jobs, and how valuable an asset in all walks of life is knowledge of people, of local conditions, and special circumstances."[36]

This knowledge, which by its nature can't be summed up in a statistic, doesn't exist in a single place for a central planner to use in his calculations. Instead, it's dispersed among millions of people who wouldn't be able to communicate it even if there were a calculus sophisticated enough to make use of it all.

Economic knowledge dispersed among people also captures realities that are—like the starlings—constantly changing.

Think about all the decisions that have to be made to produce something as simple as a loaf of bread. The farmers have to decide what kinds of grain to plant along with what kind of machinery to buy in order to harvest the crops. The bakers have to decide what kinds of ovens to use and which kinds of bread to make. The shipping companies have to decide which kinds of trucks or rail cars to use to ship the product. Wholesalers have to know how much bread to purchase from factories and retailers have to know how much they need to purchase from the wholesalers. And now add the complexity of the plastic used to wrap the loaves, which begins as oil drilled from the earth.

In a free market, there's a simple way to coordinate tens of thousands of people who produce millions of tons of bread every year: prices. A central planner doesn't have to tell the entire "flock" not to buy a rare item in order to prevent a shortage. Instead, individual producers will naturally respond to increased demand by raising the price of the good. This incentivizes both the consumer to buy less of the product and the producer to make more of it. Lowering prices, on the other hand, incentivizes producers to stop producing things that aren't profitable and incentivizes consumers to reduce unwanted surpluses.

In contrast to the idea of prices communicating information, Marx thought that the price of a good should reflect how much *work* went into it, and thus the price compensates the worker for his labor. To be fair to Marx, many people feel this way. It is intuitive to think that when we pay for a good or a service we are satisfying a balance that is owed for value created in the past. But this is only partly true, because prices aren't static descriptions of past behavior—even if payments rendered do compensate for value provided (which includes the labor used to create the product). Instead, prices are constantly-changing "signal devices" that send information to buyers in the same way wing positions send information to the birds in a flock.

When there is a shortage of rye, for example, the price of rye bread goes up to signal to consumers that there is a shortage. The farmer doesn't have to call the store and have the manager tell the customers, "We're low on rye, so if you all buy a lot of it then it will be gone!" Through a long chain of financial transactions, the storeowner learns from other people with localized knowledge and he then changes the price of the rye bread.

The price change signals to the consumer that rye is scarce and so more money has to be spent on each loaf to keep rye production viable. It also signals enterprising suppliers that they have an opportunity to make a profit if they spend the capital that is needed to deliver this scarce, desirable product to customers. When products stop being desirable, consumers don't have to call farmers to let them know that. Their lack of purchasing leads the storeowner to drop the price, and the producer learns that he needs to respond to this change in demand.

But without free markets and the prices that go with them, socialist planners have to make their best *guesses* about what kind of goods should be produced and what services are worth providing. Historically, this leads to the overproduction of unwanted goods and the underproduction of wanted goods. This underproduction can lead to shortages of vital products like food and medicine, as we saw in the famines and "bread lines" of the Soviet Union.

In 1982, the *New York Times* noted how the Soviet Union's official state newspaper *Pravda* claimed that Soviet collective farming was more productive than American capitalist farms. It then said, "Unfortunately for the people in the food lines, statistics [about the Soviet Union] suggest otherwise." Not even Soviet propaganda could hide the inferiority of planned economies to free ones. As the *Times* pointed out, while the U.S.S.R. suffered shortages, "The United States, with less than 5 percent of the labor force working in agriculture, keeps supermarkets stocked from one end of the country to the other and still exports nearly a third of its farm output."[37]

CAN IT EVER WORK?

There have been small social "communes" that operated effectively with this mentality, but not large socialist states. Even many of these communes experienced difficulties because socialist principles often contradict human nature (see chapter eight).

For example, when communal villages in Israel called *kibbutzim* (singular, *kibbutz*) were first implemented in 1909, children slept in communal houses and only saw their parents for a few hours a day. Couples were even discouraged from having tea kettles in their apartment for fear that it would encourage private time away from the community. *Kibbutzim* grew in popularity throughout much of the twentieth century, but since the 1970s most have fallen away from the strict communitarian guidelines that tried to impose more radical socialist principles on their members.[38]

But other small-scale socialist experiments were not as successful.

In mid-nineteenth-century America, followers of Etienne Cabet started their own *Icarian* colonies to bring his utopian dream to life. One of these colonies, in Iowa, housed a dozen families and became the longest-running non-religious commune in American history. Property was owned communally and decisions were made collectively. But the colonies never grew because the children ended up leaving.[39] Religious monasteries can make communal life sustainable only, it seems, because they're small and made up of adults who freely join them (and are driven by convictions other than socialism).

"Fine," a critic may say, "Maybe we have to allow people to have private property, and the ability to exchange goods on the market, but isn't there a kind of socialism that still looks out for the poor in the midst of the free market?"

We will address that question in the next chapter; but you should know that the Church has been aware of this kind of "moderate socialism" and still rejects it. Pope Pius XI said, "Such just demands and desire have nothing in them now which is inconsistent with Christian truth, and much less are they special to socialism. Those who work solely toward such ends have, therefore, no reason to become socialists" (*Quadragesimo Anno* 115).

IT'S IMPORTANT TO REMEMBER . . .

- Socialism is inherently flawed because it relies on human beings not acting as they naturally do: in favor of their own self-interest.

- Socialism's mandated equality in wealth cannot incentivize people to do the most difficult or necessary jobs.

- Central planners can never access the knowledge that is necessary to determine the amount and variety of goods and services to produce, which inevitably leads to shortages.

4
WHAT ABOUT DEMOCRATIC SOCIALISM?

A 1949 Gallup poll asked Americans, "What is your understanding of the term *socialism*?" The majority answer, at 34 percent, was "state control of business." Today, only 17 percent of people identify socialism in this way. The most popular answer in 2019, comprising 33 percent of respondents, was an identification of socialism with "equality" and government provision of benefits and social services.[40]

There have always been people who tried to achieve socialism's goals without relying on its radical methods. These socialists wanted to end poverty, but they were skeptical about using a large, central government established through a people's revolt in order to do it. Tellingly, those who did believe in that method, like Marx's partner Friedrich Engels, were immediately suspicious of their "democratic" opponents:

> These democratic socialists are either proletarians who are not yet sufficiently clear about the conditions of the liberation of their class, or they are representatives of the petty bourgeoisie, a class which, prior to the achievement of democracy and the socialist measures to which it gives rise, has many interests in common with the proletariat.[41]

Democratic socialists in the nineteenth century formed labor parties in European countries that pushed for worker reforms instead of worker revolutions, and many of them still exist today. Democratic socialists are also a rising force in American politics, and in order to see if their brand of socialism is compatible with Catholicism we need to examine their early-twentieth-century roots.

THE RISE OF DEMOCRATIC SOCIALISM

"Fighting friends" is a good way to describe the relationship between socialist playwright George Bernard Shaw and former-socialist-turned-Catholic G.K. Chesterton.[42] The duo's dissimilarities even appeared in their looks and diets: Chesterton was a hefty lover of pubs whereas Shaw was a trim vegetarian and teetotaler.

In their 1929 debate on socialism, Chesterton said that Shaw didn't *really* believe that the "community" should own the means of production. Under his model of a socialist state, "It is a few oligarchs or a few officials who do in fact control all the means of production." Chesterton went on:

> It is easy enough to say property should be distributed, but who is, as it were, the subject of the verb? Who or what is to distribute? Now it is based on the idea that the central power which condescends to distribute will be permanently just, wise, sane, and representative of the conscience of the community which has created it. That is what we doubt.[43]

Dorothy Day, the founder of the twentieth-century Catholic Worker Movement, was well-known in socialist circles but, like Chesterton, was skeptical of government assistance in ending poverty. For example, she stood against "all dictatorships, fascist and Bolshevist [communist]" and also opposed government entitlement programs like Social Security.[44] In 1944 she called that program "a great defeat for Christianity" and often quoted St. Hilary of Poitiers who said, "The less we ask of Caesar, the less we will have to render to Caesar."[45] She preferred promoting her houses of hospitality, where Catholic Workers practiced being "poor with the poor."

Modern democratic socialists usually don't sound like Dorothy Day because their beliefs come from her disciple Michael Harrington, who left the Catholic Worker Movement in the 1950s. Harrington had described it as "as far left as you could go within the Church,"[46] and soon he left the Church, too—to become an atheist, the author of a best-selling book on poverty called *The Other America*, and the founder of the Democratic Socialists of America (DSA). He believed capitalism was in the process of dying out and it was necessary to rescue the teachings of Karl Marx from authoritarian Communists who had perverted them.

Instead of a centralized economy, like what existed in the Soviet Union, Harrington argued for a "decentralized, face-to-face participation of the direct producers and their communities."[47] The current platform of the modern DSA says that since "we are unlikely to see an immediate end to capitalism tomorrow, DSA fights for reforms today that will weaken the power of corporations and increase the power of working people."[48]

And instead of replacing markets with "an all-powerful government bureaucracy," the DSA believes that "social ownership could take many forms, such as worker-owned co-operatives or publicly owned enterprises managed by workers and consumer representatives." In an interview with National Public Radio, one DSA chapter founder gave this analogy to explain how a "worker cooperative" would achieve social ownership in a way that is superior to corporate capitalism:

Let's say you were negotiating at a bargaining table with workers in a bakery, and the workers said, "Look, we want more than a quarter of the bread; we want half of the bread, or we want two-thirds of the bread." The socialist would say, "Actually, we want the bakery. We want to control it all, for all of our benefit."[49]

SOCIAL WELFARE VS. SOCIALISM

Some defenders of democratic socialism don't stress this anti-corporate mentality and simply focus on government entitlement programs. Neal Meyer, a contributor to *Jacobin* and a member of the New York City Democratic Socialists of America, says democratic socialists simply "want to build a world where everyone has a right to food, health care, a good home, an enriching education, and a union job that pays well."[50]

No one disputes that governments have a moral duty to make sure citizens have the ability to access the basic goods of life like food, education, and medicine. But *how* the access to those goods is provided is something that people can debate, and some ways of providing it are contrary to Catholic social doctrine.

When it comes to "democratic socialism," for instance, a Catholic can advocate for policies that cohere with Catholic social teaching—like a preferential option for the poor or the right of laborers to form a union. But Catholics cannot pursue policies that result in "de facto socialism" even if it's called something else. Pope St. John Paul II, for example, was aware of proposals like Meyer's that argue for the universal right to "a union job that pays well." He said in response that "the state could not directly ensure the right to work for all its citizens unless it controlled every aspect of economic life and restricted the free initiative of individuals."

Government can provide benefits to people through *social welfare programs,* like food stamps or education grants, and people are free to gauge and debate the effectiveness and value of such programs. John Paul II warned, though, that if the "welfare state" grew too large it would result in "a loss of human energies and an inordinate increase of public agencies, which are dominated more by bureaucratic ways of thinking than by concern for serving their clients, and which are accompanied by an enormous increase in spending" (*Centesimus Annus* 48).

In contrast to *social welfare* programs, the government could provide these goods directly, through socialist programs like government-run schools, hospitals, and grocery stores. Since socialism is often gradually introduced to societies through public policy, though, Catholics should approach with a healthy dose of skepticism government policies that seek to nationalize entire industries.

Of course, the existence of some nationalized industries does not mean a country has embraced full-fledged socialism. For example, having government-run schools in the United States does not mean we are a socialist country like the Soviet Union . . . though that wasn't for a lack of trying.

In 1922, Oregon tried to outlaw private and religious schools, and it was only a 1925 Supreme Court decision that kept the state from winning a monopoly on education. Pope Pius XI quoted this decision in *Divnii Illius Magistri* when he wrote, "The child is not the mere creature of the state" (37). Contrast this with Engels, who dreamed of a time when "the care and education of the children becomes a public affair; society looks after all children alike."[51]

In the United States, government on many levels provides many health care services. Yet a fully socialist health care system—an idea that more political candidates are beginning to float and more voters entertain—would be another example of central planning that should concern

Catholics. Not least of reasons why is the moral threat. If government has the only say over what services a hospital offers, then Catholic hospitals (to whatever extent they could remain identifiably so) could be mandated to provide contraception and to perform sterilizations, abortions, and so-called "sex-reassignment" surgeries, among other morally objectionable things.[52] There would also be concerns about the state's rationing of health care, potentially denying certain ordinary treatments to disabled patients and imposing euthanasia in their place.[53]

If the only alternative were cooperation with state-mandated immoral practices, the result could be the dissolution of the Catholic health care system—similar to how many Catholic adoption services have shut down rather than comply with legal mandates to facilitate adoptions to same-sex couples, but with far wider-ranging effects.

Tempting though the idea may be to some, it's hard to see how Catholics can create, in Meyer's words, "a democratic road to socialism."[54] The Church's condemnations against socialism would have remained the same even if Lenin, Mao, Pol Pot, and other socialist leaders had been elected through a democratic process.

As we will see in the sections to come, socialism is evil in principle because it deprives people of their natural rights and treats them as products of the state to be sculpted and used instead of creations of God to be dignified and respected. Furthermore, socialism is unworkable because it doesn't "see the world as it really is" and, as a result, leads to physical evils like food shortages and the abject neglect of natural resources and environments. The physical and moral evils of socialism will become clear as we examine the history of both socialism and the Catholic Church's response to it.

IT'S IMPORTANT TO REMEMBER . . .

- Socialism is not the same thing as social welfare.
  Government can provide benefits to citizens without
  banning free markets and centrally planning entire
  economies.

- Catholics cannot support the establishment of socialist
  policies even through democratic means.

PART TWO

THE BIRTH OF

SOCIALISM

5
THE FALSE
"FIRST SOCIALISTS"

Some people say Catholics not only can be socialists, they *should* be socialists because that was how the first Christians lived. David Bentley Hart says the book of Acts describes how Christians "affirmed their new faith by living in a single dwelling, selling their fixed holdings, redistributing their wealth 'as each needed,' and owning all possessions communally."[55] Jose Mena assures us that "no God-fearing Christian would want to condemn the apostolic Communism described in Acts 2 and 4."[56]

Others say socialism comes straight from Jesus himself, as can be seen in Barbara Ehrenreich's description of Jesus as a "wine-guzzling vagrant and precocious socialist."[57] Erika Christakis argues in *Time* that "Jesus would advocate a tax rate somewhere between 50 percent (in the vein of, 'If you have two coats, give one to the man who has none') and 100 percent (if you want to get into heaven, be poor). Mostly, he suggested giving all your money up for the benefit of others."[58]

But when we examine the biblical and historical evidence, a different picture emerges: the first Christians lived in communities that practiced *voluntary charity* rather than mandatory Communism.

WAS JESUS A SOCIALIST?

As Trent has argued in his previous book *Counterfeit Christs*, Jesus was not a socialist because he did not seek to either abolish private property or centralize wealth redistribution.[59] Jesus commanded people to give money to the poor (Luke 12:33), but he never specified whether that money should be given directly to the poor, donated to charities, or be taxed and redistributed though government programs.

St. Luke even describes how a person following Jesus said to him, "Teacher, bid my brother divide the inheritance with me." Instead of helping this man "redistribute wealth" Jesus answered him, "Man, who made me a judge or divider over you?" Jesus then said to the crowd following him, "Take heed, and beware of all covetousness; for a man's life does not consist in the abundance of his possessions" (Luke 12:13–15).

But if that's true, why did Jesus criticize the rich and say in Matthew 19:24 that it was easier for a camel to pass through the eye of a needle than for a rich man to enter heaven?

In the first century, ordinary people could grow or acquire only enough food to meet their basic needs, and any surplus was shared with relatives or kin who were not so well off. The rich in Jesus' time were seen as hoarders whose excess consumption directly contributed to everyone else's poverty. That's why Jesus condemned the "rich fool" who stored up resources in his barns instead of putting them to use to help others (Luke 12:16–21). As a Mediterranean proverb declares, "Every rich man is a thief or the son of a thief."[60]

But this does not mean that Jesus wanted every rich person (much less every person) to give away all he owned.

When Jesus agreed to dine with the diminutive tax collector Zacchaeus, the man said, "Behold, Lord, the half of my goods I give to the poor; and if I have defrauded any one of anything, I restore it fourfold" (Luke 19:8). Instead of saying, "Half isn't good enough! Sell *everything* and follow me," Jesus said, "Today salvation has come to this house" (Luke 19:9).

Zacchaeus and other wealthy disciples of Jesus, like Joseph of Arimathea (who could afford an expensive rock tomb for Jesus' burial), show that it is not impossible for the rich to inherit the kingdom of God—as long as they do not serve money instead of God (Matt. 6:24) or let a "love of money" become the root of their evils (1 Tim. 6:10).

WERE THE FIRST CHRISTIANS SOCIALISTS?

The second chapter of the Acts of the Apostles records how Peter's first sermon after the Jewish festival of Pentecost (which Jews call *Shavuot*) resulted in 3,000 people being baptized and joining the fledgling Christian church. The Jewish historian Josephus and St. Luke, the author of Acts, confirm that many of the visitors to Jerusalem at this time were pilgrims from all over the Roman Empire. But instead of returning home after the festival, these new converts "devoted themselves to the apostles' teaching and fellowship, to the breaking of bread and the prayers" (Acts 2:42).

The early Church now had a "blessing of a problem" on its hands. These visitors needed help finding a place to live and a way to sustain themselves. Fortunately, the Christian community in Jerusalem responded generously so that "all who believed were together and had all things in common; and they sold their possessions and goods and distributed them to all, as any had need" (Acts 2:45). But does this arrangement entail "apostolic Communism"?

First, there is doubt about whether first-century Christians completely renounced private property. Acts 2:45 uses an imperfect verb to say of their possessions, "They were selling and were dividing them to all" (in Greek, *hyparxeis epipraskon kai diemerizon auta*) instead of saying in the simple past tense, "They sold and distributed them to all." This seems to describe a *continuing* process of selling extra property and goods in order to support the poor. But in order to do that, Christians would have had to retain some property even after becoming believers.

Moreover, although the New Testament contains many commands to help the poor, it does not contain any commands for believers to give up their possessions to communal ownership. If that were the case, we would expect the biblical authors to discuss the issue of tithing, or required giving. But as New Testament scholar Craig Blomberg points out, although tithing was commanded of God's people in the Old Testament, "no New Testament text ever mandates a tithe but rather commands generous and sacrificial giving instead."[61]

This can be seen in St. Paul's petition to the Corinthians that they give to a collection for poor believers in Judea. Paul never commanded them to do this but instead he hoped it would be seen "not as an exaction but as a willing gift. . . . Each one must do as he has made up his mind, not reluctantly or under compulsion, for God loves a cheerful giver" (2 Cor. 9:5,7).

But even if the first Christians renounced some or all of their private property, that doesn't mean every Christian is bound to do the same. There is a difference between a *description* of what some Christians did and a *prescription* of what all Christians ought to do.

For example, the New Testament describes Christians meeting in private homes for worship (1 Cor. 16:19), but that doesn't mean it is wrong for Christians to worship in churches today. Likewise, the description of Christians selling property and bringing the proceeds to the apostles' feet for communal distribution (Acts 4:34–35) doesn't mean this behavior was a moral requirement for all believers then—or is now.

In response, critics like Hart contend that the story of Ananias and Sapphira shows that renouncing property and giving it to the apostles was mandatory because the couple was struck down for withholding their property from the collection. But a careful reading of the passage shows that the couple's sin was not their mere withholding of property. Peter says the property was theirs before they sold it and they would have retained their right to use it even after selling it (Acts 5:4). Rather, it was their lie to the apostles who represented God's authority that incurred the fatal judgment against them.

WAS THE EARLY CHURCH SOCIALIST?

Ancient pagan critics like Lucian and Christian apologists like Justin Martyr both attest to Christians living a common life together and sharing what they had with one another.[62] This isn't surprising, given that by the second century Jews who worshipped Jesus had been expelled from the synagogues and the Romans often persecuted people who openly admitted to being Christian. In the absence of civil or religious support, Christians relied on one another to survive.

But there's no reason why we must infer from this communal living was or is essential to the Christian faith. The prescription for us may be more general. As Pope Benedict XVI notes, "As the Church grew, this radical form of material communion could not in fact be preserved. But its essential core remained: within the community of believers there can never be room for a poverty that denies anyone what is needed for a dignified life" (*Deus Caritas Est* 20).

As Christians became more accepted in the Roman Empire, reports of their generosity preceded them. The Roman emperor Julian the Apostate even griped about how Christians "support not only their own poor but ours as well; all men see that our people lack aid from us."[63] Once Roman persecution ended, some Christians were able to climb the social ladder and achieve wealth, which they were not required to renounce but could prudently manage instead.

Hart claims that the early Christians always condemned the accumulation of wealth; and some of them, like Ambrose, did—when it was not put to good use in serving the poor. But Hart goes further when he claims that the Church Fathers condemned the possession of wealth *itself* regardless of how it's used. He asserts "The great John Chrysostom frequently issued pronouncements on wealth and poverty that make Karl Marx and Mikhail Bakunin sound like timid conservatives."[64] But from Marx's perspective, Chrysostom probably sounded like an enemy of the socialist cause when he wrote:

> A rich man is one thing, a rapacious man is another: an affluent man is one thing, a covetous man is another. Make clear distinctions, and do not confuse things which are diverse. Are you a rich man? I forbid you not. Are you a rapacious man? I denounce you. Have you property of your own? Enjoy it. Do you take the property of others? I will not hold my peace.[65]

In the centuries after the fall of Rome in A.D. 476, invading northern tribes, plagues, and poor crop yields decimated the European population. Apart from a few Christian monasteries that preserved ancient knowledge, what remained were powerful local rulers whose wealth consisted of land they owned and the peasants, called *serfs,* who were subject to them (a system we call *feudalism*).

Today, serfdom is considered on par with slavery, but in the Middle Ages it was considered a moral improvement because whereas slaves had the same value as livestock, serfs were recognized as persons made in the image of God.[66] As persons they were baptized and had rights their feudal lord had to respect, though they did not have meaningful freedom. They were forced to farm for a lord (or one of his vassals), who in return provided them with food, shelter, and protection. And, unlike slaves, serfs could own property and keep some of what they produced.

This is important because the concept of serfdom will be referenced both in the arguments of the true "first socialists" of the nineteenth century and in the writings of their twentieth-century critics. The latter claimed that socialism does not move humanity forward to a utopian ideal but that it takes it backward on a ruinous "road to serfdom" that turns the state into the new lord, making the rest of us its servants.

IT'S IMPORTANT TO REMEMBER . . .

- Jesus required his followers to help the poor, but he did not tell them to support government confiscation and allocation of wealth.

- The early Church practiced charity but did not require believers to renounce private property or support what we would now call socialism.

6
THE REAL
"FIRST SOCIALISTS"

Around the corner from the Louvre in Paris is the small Café de la Régence, a haven for chess players both literal and metaphorical. On an August afternoon in 1844, two German twenty-somethings, Karl Marx and Friedrich Engels, sat among these players for lunch.

Engels had just come from working at a mill in England where his parents had sent him in hopes he would abandon his radical philosophies. Instead, the poverty and filthy conditions he witnessed in the mill towns motivated him to write *The Condition of the Working Class in England*. This confirmed Marx's belief that history was just one long story about the rich oppressing the poor, but this time factory owners took the place of feudal lords or Roman slave drivers.

There had been self-identified socialists before Marx, but they were "utopian dreamers" who hoped the rich would adopt their elaborate plans for a better world.[67] Marx and Engels, in contrast, believed that a just society was achieved not by persuading kings and queens but by equipping the pawns to overthrow them. And so, in 1848, they published *The Communist Manifesto*, which declared, "Let the ruling classes tremble at a Communistic revolution. The proletarians (poor workers) have nothing to lose but their chains. They have a world to win."[68]

We can't understand the first socialists, though, unless we understand the capitalism they rejected. And we can't understand capitalism unless we examine it at its origins in fourteenth-century Italy.

TRADING FEUDALISM FOR CAPITALISM

If you were glancing over Leonardo Da Vinci's desk as he painted *The Last Supper,* you might have seen this reminder in one of his notebooks: "Learn multiplication from the root from *Maestro* Luca." If Da Vinci was history's most famous inventor, then his friend, the Franciscan friar Luca Pacioli, was its most famous accountant. You have probably never heard of him, but his mathematics textbook has been called "the most influential book on capitalism" ever written.[69]

To see why, we need to return to the issue of trade.

You'll recall that serfs could own some property; but it was always meager and what their property produced was primarily traded with relatives. Some could amass enough goods to sell at local fairs, but no one got rich with this kind of trading. That began to change in the thirteenth and fourteenth centuries when mercantile capitalists like Marco Polo began transporting large numbers of goods from locations where they were cheap over long distances in order to sell them in places where they were expensive.

Other merchants wanted these profits without personally making a 7,000-mile trek into China, so they formed companies that provided the money (or *capital*) to fund these trading expeditions. The investors in these "joint-stock" companies would receive returns from successful expeditions and share the losses from unsuccessful ones, thereby minimizing risk and encouraging more investors to join the company. As more investors joined, companies were able to use some of their profit to grow their enterprise.

Markets had always existed in one form or another since antiquity, but now wealth could be *created* instead of just being discovered, and that meant it could be reinvested to create more wealth. Hence, *capitalism* (in the nascent form of "merchant capitalism") was born.

As these companies grew and global trade increased, there came to be a shortage in precious metals like gold and silver that were used to mint coins. In addition, transporting coins became a hazardous way of moving wealth because caravans could be robbed and ships often sank. Banks became a safer place to deposit wealth because a person could deposit coins in one area and then withdraw the same amount in another area through a banknote. But while a local, traveling merchant only had to keep track of how many coins were in his purse, trading companies had to keep track of hundreds or even thousands of transactions taking place across different continents.

And that's where Da Vinci's friend Master Luca enters the picture.

Two years after Columbus discovered the New World and opened up even more trading opportunities, Pacioli published a summary of mathematics that included instructions for performing "double-entry book keeping." This method of accounting requires two entries for every transaction: one for the debited account on the left side of the ledger and one for the credited account on the right. Both columns should add up to the same amount, which helps prevent errors and allows for more complex transactions.

Jewish merchants had used this tidy method for centuries, but the printing press made Pacioli's description of it accessible to a growing class of entrepreneurs who were leading an economic revolution.

For the first time in human history, wealth was not something that belonged solely to lords who merely inherited it from other's labor. Now men like Josiah Wedgwood could create wealth through their ingenuity and effort. Wedgewood grew up in poverty as the youngest of thirteen children, but by the middle of the eighteenth century he had started a pottery business that eventually produced affordable ceramics for palaces and humble homes alike. He advertised pottery as "Queen's Ware" and pioneered the use of retail methods like catalogues and money-back guarantees.[70] Wedgewood was also an abolitionist who fought the slave trade and saw businesses that used efficient mass production as the moral alternative to slavery. The expansion of private business also drove down the cost of goods so that the average person could have access to goods that once belonged only to royalty.

This was true not just of Wedgewood's pottery but also of basic necessities like bread, milk, meat, and medicine, the wider availability of which vastly improved the quality of life—and the span of life—for all workers. For example, it took tens of thousands of years for the global population to reach 600 million by the year 1700. But in just a hundred years the population grew to 900 million, and by the year 1900 it had hit 1.65 billion.[71] In other words, thanks to economic advancements, hundreds of millions of people reached adulthood and had families of their own who would have otherwise died young of starvation or disease.

CAPITALISM'S MELANCHOLY MADNESS

As cities expanded to accommodate rapidly growing businesses, the resulting influx of people led to crowded, unsanitary, and dangerous places. In his 1854 novel *Hard Times,* Charles Dickens describes a fictional version of Manchester, England called Coketown, whose red bricks had become choked by smoke and ash from the numerous mills. He writes, "It had a black canal in it, and a river that ran purple with ill-smelling dye, and vast piles of building full of windows where there was a rattling and a trembling all day long, and where the piston of the steam-engine worked monotonously up and down, like the head of an elephant in a state of melancholy madness."[72]

Engels echoed Dickens descriptions of the town's "measureless filth and stench" and described it as disease-ridden and indicative of how the poor "must really have reached the lowest stage of humanity."[73] Engels also believed that workers had better wages and quality of life before the Industrial Revolution when they worked on farms.[74] Marx and Engels predicted in *The Communist Manifesto* that English workers would no longer tolerate this oppression and would rise up against their capitalist overlords. But the revolution never came, partly because the English government passed laws that restricted child labor, regulated workplaces, and improved public sanitation.

A similar episode took place in the U.S. five decades later, when Upton Sinclair published installments of his novel *The Jungle* in a socialist newspaper in 1905. It depicted the grim conditions of Chicago meatpacking plants through a fictional story about a Lithuanian immigrant named Jurgis Rudkus. Sinclair's descriptions of the plants are like a trip through Dante's inferno where workers endure unique, hellish conditions based on their tasks rather than their sins. For example, some men get their fingernails peeled off as they prepare meat while others fall into steam vats and have their remains turned into lard.[75]

The American author Jack London called Sinclair's book "the *Uncle Tom's Cabin* of wage slavery" and Sinclair hoped it would spark a socialist revolution in the same way that that book helped ignite the Civil War.[76] But the book's most notable accomplishment was spurring passage of the 1906

Pure Food and Drug Act, which created what is now known as the Food and Drug Administration. Food was now safer, but socialism now seemed less attainable: a fact Sinclair noted when he said of his book, "I aimed at the public's heart, and by accident I hit it in the stomach."[77]

CAPITALISM'S GREATEST SIN

Although inhuman working conditions (which the Church also condemned along with socialism) played a part in socialist arguments, they were not socialism's primary complaint. Instead, the greatest injustice of capitalism was that workers depended on wages from capitalists and they were cheated out of the wages they truly deserved.

Engels said that having to earn a wage at all put workers "in the most revolting, inhuman position conceivable for a human being." He even claimed that slaves and serfs were better off than nineteenth-century lower-class workers:

> The slave is assured of a bare livelihood by the self-interest of his master, the serf has at least a scrap of land on which to live; each has at worst a guarantee for life itself. But the proletarian must depend upon himself alone, and is yet prevented from so applying his abilities as to be able to rely upon them.[78]

Marx further protested the fact that mass-production techniques multiplied worker productivity but worker compensation did not increase at the same rate. He concluded that capitalists were stealing this "surplus value" of a worker's labor and calling it profit. Marx argued instead for a "labor value" of a worker's labor that an employee could redeem from a "socially owned" source of income based on how long or hard he worked.[79] But in order to do this, capitalists would have to be stripped of their means of production and prevented from retaining profits that belonged to their employees.

At the same time Marx and Engels published *The Communist Manifesto*, revolutions were breaking out across Europe, overthrowing constitutional monarchies in places like France, Denmark, and Hungary and establishing a free press and parliamentary governments in their place. A few decades later, labor riots broke out in America and socialists captured the city of Paris and ruled it for nearly two weeks.[80] All this prompted Pope Leo XIII to write an encyclical on these "new things," in which he acknowledged that "the discussion is not easy, nor is it void of danger" because there are "crafty agitators" who "pervert men's judgments and to stir up the people to revolt."

Even still, the pope defended his foray into politics and economics in *Rerum Novarum* because "the responsibility of the apostolic office urges us to treat the question of set purpose and in detail, in order that no misapprehension may exist as to the principles which truth and justice dictate for its settlement" (2).

IT'S IMPORTANT TO REMEMBER . . .

- The rise of capitalism led to an increase in wealth, but at the cost of dangerous jobs and an increase in urban squalor.

- Early socialists seized on these social injustices to argue that capitalism itself needed to be abandoned in order to protect the dignity of workers.

7
LEO XIII ON PRIVATE PROPERTY

The French philosopher Jean-Jacques Rousseau said ownership of land was a lie because "the fruits of the earth belong to us all, and the earth itself to nobody."[81] This means anyone who owns property must have stolen it from someone else, a sentiment the anarchist Pierre Proudhon expressed in the famous slogan *La propriété, c'est le vol!* or "Property is theft!"[82]

The Church does not share their rejection of private property, even if Catholic doctrines like the *universal destination of goods* can be twisted to sound like socialism. That's why Pope Leo XIII begins his critique of socialism in *Rerum Novarum* by saying, "It is surely undeniable that, when a man engages in remunerative labor, the impelling reason and motive of his work is to obtain property, and thereafter to hold it as his very own" (5).

THE RIGHT TO ACQUIRE PROPERTY AND WEALTH

The primary reason that people work in exchange for money (what's called *remunerative labor*) is so that they can use that money to obtain their own property. Leo writes, "If one man hires out to another his strength or skill, he does so for the purpose of receiving in return what is necessary for the satisfaction of his needs." This does not mean the man *only* has a right to an income that satisfies his basic needs, though, because Leo goes on to say that this worker "expressly intends to acquire a right full and real, not only to the remuneration, but also to the disposal of such remuneration, just as he pleases" (5).

The right to acquire money through work would be no right at all if you had to surrender all of what you earned to the state (and thus weren't free to spend it "as you please"). In addition, a person's right to wages includes the right to convert those wages into property that remains under his control. That way, "If he lives sparingly, saves money, and, for greater security, invests his savings in land, the land, in such case, is only his wages under another form; and, consequently, a working man's little estate thus purchased should be as completely at his full disposal as are the wages he receives for his labor."

Leo concludes that socialists "deprive [a worker] of the liberty of disposing of his wages, and thereby of all hope and possibility of increasing his resources and of bettering his condition in life" (5). Elsewhere, in his letter on socialism, he says they

> assail the right of property sanctioned by natural law; and by a scheme of horrible wickedness, while they seem desirous of caring for the needs and satisfying the desires of all men, they strive to seize and hold in common whatever has been acquired either by title of lawful inheritance, or by labor of brain and hands, or by thrift in one's mode of life (*Quod Apostolici Muneris* 1).

Notice that Leo did not condemn socialism because it was necessarily atheistic or authoritarian. Rather, he condemned socialism because of its lack of respect toward the *natural right to private property*.

ALL FOR ONE AND ONE FOR ALL

The claim that "property is theft" is nonsensical, because you can only "steal" what someone else rightfully owns. Even Karl Marx said that "'theft' as a forcible violation of property presupposes the existence of property."[83] In fact, there is no contradiction between publicly available goods and private ownership of those goods.

Leo responds to critics like Rousseau who say people have the right to *use* the land but they don't have the right to *own* it by saying "they are defrauding man of what his own labor has produced." That's because "the soil which is tilled and cultivated with toil and skill utterly changes its condition; it was wild before, now it is fruitful; was barren, but now brings forth in abundance." And because man has used his God-given abilities to transform the earth into a resource, "it cannot but be just that he should possess that portion as his very own, and have a right to hold it without any one being justified in violating that right" (*Rerum Novarum* 9).

Leo's argument for private property also rests on the ability to carry out our moral duties. If you have the duty of filling my car with gasoline, it follows you have the right to drive my car, because you can't carry out the former duty without the latter ability. Likewise, if we have a duty to carry on lives that, unlike other animals, have stability and focus on pursuing the good, then "it must be within [man's] right to possess things not merely for temporary and momentary use, as other living things do, but to have and to hold them in stable and permanent possession" (6).

This is "all the stronger" for families because "it is a most sacred law of nature that a father should provide food and all necessaries for those whom he has begotten." If parents have a duty to provide for their dependents, they must have a way to provide for these people. Leo goes on to say, "In no other way can a father effect this except by the ownership of productive property, which he can transmit to his children by inheritance." This stands in contrast to Marx's call to abolish not just the law of inheritance but the family itself (which we'll examine in more detail in chapter ten).

Leo is adamant that it is not the state's responsibility to provide for individuals or their families, except in extreme situations of poverty.[84] "There is no need to bring in the state" because "man precedes the state, and possesses, prior to the formation of any state, the right of providing for the substance of his body." Likewise, the duty of parents to provide for their children "can be neither abolished nor absorbed by the state," and when socialists seek to give the state the parents' duty to provide for children, they "act against natural justice, and destroy the structure of the home" (14).

A century before the birth of Christ, the Roman statesman Cicero defended the right to property by comparing it to the seats in a theater: "Though the theater is a public place, yet it is correct to say that the particular seat a man has taken belongs to him, so in the state or in the universe, though these are common to all, no principle of justice militates against the possession of private property."[85] Likewise, Pope Leo says, "The fact that God has given the earth for the use and enjoyment of the whole human race can in no way be a bar to the owning of private property" (8).

In fact, one way the earth serves the whole human race is through individual owners of property who convert what they own into goods (like crops or steel) that serve everyone else's needs. As economies advance, the labor that creates these goods becomes more specialized and allows for more resources to be produced and distributed throughout the world, including to the poor.

In 2015, YouTuber Andy George tried to make a chicken sandwich from scratch, literally. He acquired a chicken, grew his own wheat and vegetable garden, built a press to turn sunflower seeds into vegetable oil, and even traveled to the ocean to procure salt. It took six months and $1,500 to make a chicken sandwich that didn't taste very good.[86] But you can go to a fast-food restaurant and get a delicious chicken sandwich at .0003 percent of the cost and in .00003 percent of the time—all thanks to the good of private property, the division of specialized labor, and free markets where property can be sold in order to benefit other people.

THE GOOD OF PRIVATE PROPERTY

In his 1776 work "Wealth of Nations," Adam Smith said a nation's wealth wasn't found in the gold within a king's vault. Instead, its wealth existed in its citizens' having a high standard of living because of their ability to freely trade their goods and services. As these individuals acquire wealth for themselves, they also indirectly create wealth for the community as a whole through their unique trades. Or, as Smith puts it, "It is not from the benevolence of the butcher, the brewer, or the baker that we expect our dinner, but from their regard to their own interest."[87]

That's one reason why Leo says socialism isn't just immoral; it's impossible. He warns that if socialism were adopted, "The door would be thrown open to envy, to mutual invective, and to discord; the sources of wealth themselves would run dry, for no one would have any interest in exerting his talents or his industry" (*Rerum Novarum* 15).

Leo was well-aware of that most basic incentive problem we covered in chapter three: getting people to work.

He saw that without the opportunity for real and personal gain through wage labor and the accumulation of private property (i.e., thrift and savings), few men would work with enough industriousness to ensure a level of prosperity conducive to peace.

But when people like bakers and brewers exert their talents, they can end up acquiring more property than others. Socialists believe this inequality is a problem to be remedied through the communal production of wealth that is equally distributed to everyone. However, as we will show in the subsequent chapters, Pope Leo XIII was correct when he said, "That ideal equality about which they entertain pleasant dreams would be in reality the leveling down of all to a like condition of misery and degradation" (15).

IT'S IMPORTANT TO REMEMBER . . .

- God gave the earth to all of humanity (this is the *universal destination of goods*), but this does not preclude individuals from rightfully owning parts of the world and using it for good purposes.

- The Church teaches that socialism is wrong because it denies man's natural right both to acquire wealth and property and to dispose of them as he pleases.

- Socialism is flawed because it fails to see that private property allows people to carry out their moral duties to one another, such as by providing for one's family or creating goods and services for one's fellow man.

8
LEO XIII AND HUMAN NATURE

In 1924, nineteen-year-old Nathan Leopold and eighteen-year-old Richard Loeb lured fourteen-year-old Bobby Franks into their car, where they stabbed him repeatedly in the head with a chisel before dumping the body in a ditch by some railroad tracks near Chicago. The duo were wealthy and intelligent and seemed to have no motive for the killing. So their attorney, the famous Clarence Darrow, convinced the judge to spare them the death penalty by arguing that the crime wasn't really their fault. "Somewhere in the infinite processes that go to the making up of the boy or the man," he said, "something slipped, and those unfortunate lads sit here hated, despised, outcasts, with the community shouting for their blood."[88]

Darrow's defense relied on a belief about human nature shared by many socialists. Instead of being born with sinful tendencies we must overcome through virtue and grace, socialists believe we are born good, and it is societal processes or social structures that cause us to become evil. They follow Rousseau, who said, "Man is naturally good" and, "Society depraves and perverts men."[89]

Rousseau also believed that society makes us unequal because human talents and fortunes are distributed unequally. The socialist answer to this "unnatural inequality" is mandated equality, which is why the Communist Party of the Soviet Union declared in 1986, "Communism is a classless social system with one form of public ownership of the means of production and with full social equality of all members of society."[90] But in *Rerum Novarum,* Pope Leo XIII says this is backward because "it is impossible to reduce civil society to one dead level. Socialists may in that intent do their utmost, but all striving against nature is in vain" (*Rerum Novarum*, 17).

UNEQUAL ISN'T UNFAIR

For socialists, "equality" isn't just a matter of providing people with equal *opportunities* (like equal standing under the law). Instead, true equality can only be achieved through mandating equal *outcomes*. In 1913, the eminent socialist Bernard Shaw wrote, "Socialism, translated into concrete terms, means equal division of the national income among all the inhabitants of the country."[91]

Human beings are certainly equal with regard to their basic rights and dignity, because God made us that way. But we can never be equal in things like wealth, health, or accomplishments because, as Leo observes, "There naturally exist among mankind manifold differences of the most important kind; people differ in capacity, skill, health, strength; and unequal fortune is a necessary result of unequal condition." And whereas Rousseau would consider this situation a defect in need of a remedy, Leo says,

> Such inequality is far from being disadvantageous either to individuals or to the community. Social and public life can only be maintained by means of various kinds of capacity for business and the playing of many parts; and each man, as a rule, chooses the part which suits his own peculiar domestic condition (17).

Leo believed, building on the classical and Christian traditions before him, that the fact of natural differences among human beings promotes the distinct good of *needing one another* for our earthly and spiritual needs. Humans aren't identical, like interchangeable cogs in a machine or worker ants. They're more like specialized organs that work together for the good of a whole body—be it the family, the neighborhood, the nation, or the Body of Christ. These differences constitute a "glue" that holds the body together and allows us to receive genuine gifts of friendship from one another (something that would be impossible if we were all equal and already possessed those gifts).

This interdependence that springs from our inequality can be called *Christian realism*. It is realistic because it recognizes the natural differences among human beings. It is Christian in how it recognizes that some of them are good for us. For example, we could not have genuine responsibility for one another, or what is called *solidarity*, without some kind of inequality. This sentiment can be found in the writings of the twelfth-century mystic St. Catherine of Siena, who heard God tell her,

> I could easily have created men possessed of all that they should need both for body and soul, but I wish that one should have need of the other, and that they should be my ministers to administer the graces and the gifts that they have received from me. Whether man will or no, he cannot help making an act of love.[92]

THE DIGNITY OF WORK

Another unnatural aspect of socialism is its hostility to work, especially physical labor. Marx believed mental and physical labor should be divided equally among people;

his son-in-law Paul Lafargue went so far as to write in *The Right to Be Lazy* that work itself should be forbidden. He declares, "Jehovah, the bearded and angry god, gave his worshipers the supreme example of ideal laziness; after six days of work, he rests for all eternity" (though Lafargue overlooked John 5:17, where Jesus said the Father is still at work).[93]

The 2016 Tradinista! Manifesto likewise objected to the idea that "people must sell their labor-power on the market in order to survive."[94] Their solution to this injustice is found in the state's "guaranteeing a livelihood independent of the market." This sentiment was even echoed in 2019 when a summary of the "Green New Deal" claimed that the government should provide "economic security for all who are unable or *unwilling to work* [emphasis added].[95]

In other words, no one should have to work for a living. But is this natural or healthy for human beings? According to Leo XIII:

> As regards bodily labor, even had man never fallen from the state of innocence, he would not have remained wholly idle; but that which would then have been his free choice and his delight became afterward compulsory, and the painful expiation for his disobedience. "Cursed be the earth in thy work; in thy labor thou shalt eat of it all the days of thy life" (*Rerum Novarum* 17).

Simply put, bodily labor is not evil in itself. What is evil is the physical toil and pain we experience as a necessary byproduct of having corruptible bodies in a fallen world. This is why Leo says, "Nothing is more useful than to look upon the world as it really is, and at the same time to seek elsewhere, as we have said, for the solace to its troubles" (18).

That "elsewhere" is the life of grace that gives courage to bear all manner of human hardship.

This does not mean that people must accept any suffering they endure in their occupations and just wait for heaven's reprieve. Later in *Rerum Novarum,* Leo exhorts employers, "It is neither just nor human so to grind men down with excessive labor as to stupefy their minds and wear out their bodies" (42). Socialists who promise "undisturbed repose, and constant enjoyment" actually "delude the people and impose upon them, and their lying promises will only one day bring forth evils worse than the present" (18).

This warning would fit defenders of "Fully Automated Luxury Communism," such as Aaron Bastani, who promised unlimited leisure for humans while robots do all our work.[96] The DSA would no doubt agree, since they say that "a long-term goal of socialism is to eliminate all but the most enjoyable kinds of labor."[97] However, in "the world as it really is" labor, including exhausting labor both physical and mental, is a necessary and healthy part of life. Pope John Paul II said this reality affects not just traditional "hard workers" like farmers but also

> those who bear the burden of grave responsibility for decisions that will have a vast impact on society. It is familiar to doctors and nurses, who spend days and nights at their patients' bedside. It is familiar to women, who, sometimes without proper recognition on the part of society and even of their own families, bear the daily burden and responsibility for their homes and the upbringing of their children. *It is familiar to all workers* and, since work is a universal calling, it is familiar to everyone (*Laborem Exercens* 9).

He goes on to describe how "in spite of all this toil—perhaps, in a sense, because of it—work is a good thing for

73

man." That's because it allows him to excel in the virtue of industriousness and by acquiring this good he "achieves fulfillment as a human being and indeed, in a sense, becomes 'more a human being.'"

MAKING PIGS FLY

Let us sum up. According to Leo XIII, socialism is unnatural because it denies the fundamental truth that God made human beings to cultivate the earth through labor. He wants us to retain the fruits of our labor through the acquisition of property that we can use to benefit those who are dependent upon us, including by leaving it to them as an estate. The idea that the state should usurp this role from men and women and from the family is not only a "great and pernicious error" but a serious attack on natural justice (*Rerum Novarum* 14).

Moreover, socialism denies the truth that human beings, though equal in dignity, are unequal in talents, passions, and abilities. This inequality is a good thing because it's what creates the "social web" that unites all of us toward a common good. If we were all self-sufficient animals that hunt and live in solitude, then no human community would ever need to form. But man is a social animal by nature, and denying his natural desire to compete and excel does nothing to further his well-being.

Socialism is unnatural because it expects humans to ignore their natural desire to acquire property and instead to give themselves wholly over to the state. They are then expected to work even if they don't need to, and some will be expected to perform more-difficult work in exchange for the same compensation everyone else receives: access to communal rations. Those workers are then expected to care for property like a home that may be transferred at any time to a stranger at the discretion of central planners.

There has never been a socialist state in the same way there has never and will never be a flying pig: they both completely contradict nature. And, just as the only way you could make a pig fly would be to violently alter its being through surgery, the only way to make human beings conform to the socialist society is to violently intervene in their lives and compel them to live that way. That this is the case will become abundantly clear as we examine how socialism developed throughout the world after the publication of *Rerum Novarum*.

IT'S IMPORTANT TO REMEMBER . . .

- Socialism fails to account for the reality of human nature. Human beings are equal in dignity but unequal in talents and life choices.

- Socialism is wrong because it tries to equalize that which is essentially unequal (e.g., talents and abilities) and prevents human beings from charitably relying on one another because of this natural inequality.

- Work is not evil in itself, but has become burdensome because of original sin. However, human beings can redeem work by offering their bodily labor for the good of others and themselves.

PART THREE

THE RISE

OF SOCIALISM

9
SOCIALISM GETS A STATE

Marx said, "There is only one way in which the murderous death agonies of the old society and the bloody birth throes of the new society can be shortened, simplified and concentrated, and that way is revolutionary terror."[98] Marx and Engels believed this worker's revolution would take place in a highly industrialized country like England where factory workers would overthrow their capitalist overlords. But the revolution actually arrived in an economically backward part of the world: Russia.

WAR AND REVOLUTION

In 1898, industrial workers made up less than 3 percent of the Russian population, and socialists wondered how the peasant population could ever be unified to overthrow their royal rulers.[99] In 1901, Vladimir Ulyanov, a member of the Russian Social Democratic Labor party, published a pamphlet entitled *What Must Be Done?* In it he argued that a political party must lead the small working class to a socialist victory and "professional revolutionaries" would have to maintain control over these workers even after the revolution, lest they backslide into the old order.

Fearing for his personal safety, Ulyanov published the pamphlet under the pen name Vladimir Lenin and he would have to wait until 1917 before his revolutionary vision came to pass.

In that year, massive fatalities and food shortages related to Russia's involvement in World War I turned public opinion against the monarchy. Groups of workers councils, called *soviets*, led revolts in major cities, and Tsar Nicholas II abdicated the throne. Lenin returned from exile in Germany to lead the majority (or *Bolshevik*) faction of the Russian socialist party.

During this period, the Bolshevik "Red Army" enacted a policy of militant Communism, taking up civil war against the opposing "White Army" of anti-communist Russians. They banned private enterprise, nationalized industry, and confiscated grain from farmers for central planning purposes. This proved to be a disaster and contributed to a famine that killed five million people. But the Bolsheviks prevailed, and in 1922 the country was reconstituted as the Union of Soviet Socialist Republics, or U.S.S.R.

THE TEN-POUND NAIL IN THE COFFIN

In 1875, Marx had proposed that in the highest phase of Communism, "after labor has become not only a means of life but life's prime want" and automation has produced more resources than are demanded, society can live by the motto, "From each according to his ability, to each according to his needs."[100] But until then, people must live under a lower phase of Communism and would have to settle for the motto, "To each according to his contribution."

Under this view, workers would receive "labor vouchers" they could exchange for goods and services. That way, as Lenin put it, "every worker, therefore, receives from society as much as he has given to it."[101] Soviet factories and businesses were then encouraged to produce as many goods as possible so that they could be easily distributed to everyone.

But remember the knowledge problem we discussed in chapter three. No central planner can ever know the millions of variables that go into deciding when it's worthwhile to produce a good or offer a service. For example, most hardware stores carry dozens if not hundreds of different kinds of nails. How does the store know how many and what kind of nails to stock? How does the factory know what type and number of nails to produce?

The answer is that individual purchases of nails communicate *information* about each product. This information is then reflected in prices that owners set in order to maintain profits based on available supplies and consumer demand, as well as in production decisions made by nail manufacturers. Through millions of individual exchanges enough information is communicated— without any central organization—for business owners to set and, more importantly, *change* prices for all their goods and services to reflect what is going on in the market.

But unlike capitalist economies that allow *prices (and production)* to adjust according to consumer choice, the Soviet system set rigid *production targets,* and consumers just had to "choose" whatever was offered to them.

So, instead of a factory producing nails based on sales reports from retailers, the government would just tell a nail factory that 100,000 nails were needed by the end of the month. Even though socialist factories couldn't go out of business, coercive threats motivated them to meet the government's quotas, even when this led to absurd results and provided no benefit to consumers.

For example, if the government's production target was based on the number of nails the factory had to produce, then the factory could simply make 100,000 tiny, useless nails in order to quickly satisfy the quota. If, on the other hand, the target was based on the gross weight of the nails, the factory could produce ten tons of large, clunky nails that were easier to make than well-crafted nails. And, as one researcher notes: it wasn't just nails the Soviet economy had trouble producing:

> The prevalence and severity of shoddy workmanship in goods produced under the Soviet production system boggles the American mind. Factories turned out washing machines that did nothing but wet clothes, sewing machines missing essential screws, hair dryers that immediately short-circuited, and refrigerators without motors (yet Samarkand Refrigerator Factory won numerous awards and increased annual subsidies for continually exceeding its production plan).[102]

No central computer system today, much less a planning committee a century ago, could calculate the supply and demand variables for every conceivable product on the market. Even if it could, as Hayek showed, getting the knowledge for those calculations is impossible because it's dispersed across millions of producers and consumers.

Without prices, planners would need consumer surveys that relied on honest opinions that don't change in the future. For example, people may say they want more educational programming on television but end up watching (and thus paying for) reality television or cable news. That's why a socialist system of supply that is blind to demand often leads to the overproduction of useless products and the underproduction, or shortages, of vitally important products.

But if socialism is impossible, some may ask, how did the Soviet Union exist for nearly seventy years under this system?

The answer is that the Soviets could partially avoid the knowledge problem by relying on prices determined by other, market-based economies to guide their production targets. This wasn't ideal, and it still led to shortages, but it allowed the system to limp along until it finally collapsed at the end of the twentieth century. In the meantime, the economic consequences of the system were often hidden from the world, including its most horrifying consequence: the Ukrainian famine.

MURDER BY ANY OTHER NAME

In 1921, Lenin allowed people to participate in "state-controlled capitalism" (strict government oversight of private businesses) in order to get the economy on track. This resulted in some farmers getting rich and being derided as *kulaks*, from the Ukrainian for "tight fist." But in 1928, under the leadership of Lenin's successor Joseph Stalin, the Soviets launched their "Five-Year Plan" to industrialize the country and make it capable of defending itself against both foreign and domestic threats.

In the real world, a country can't just over-produce goods in order to alleviate poverty. It has to choose which resources to produce, and the Soviets focused on heavy industry at the expense of things like food production. In 1929, Stalin seized the Kulaks' assets and "liquidated" the Kulaks themselves through murder and deportation. Soviet propaganda blamed the country's food shortages on "greedy Kulaks," but the true cause were Soviet troops that confiscated livestock and grain from peasants of all classes because those materials "belonged" to the government's central planners.

The famine that swept through Ukraine between 1932–1933, killing five million, was not a natural one caused by something like a bad crop yield. It was, like the Holocaust, state-sanctioned murder. Today it is called the *Holodomor,* which means "to kill by starvation."[103] In an area that once produced the most grain in all of Europe, hunger drove desperate people to cook shoes, bones, and finally, as one observer described, "There were people who cut up corpses, who killed their own children and ate them. I saw one."[104]

Even more appalling, some Western intellectuals who supported the Soviets' policies denied the existence of the famine. George Bernard Shaw wrote to the *Manchester Guardian* after visiting the Soviet Union in 1933, "Everywhere we saw hopeful and enthusiastic working class" that provided "an example of industry and conduct which would greatly enrich us if our systems supplied our workers with any incentive to follow it."[105]

Pulitzer-prize-winning journalist Walter Duranty wrote in the *New York Times* that "any report of a famine in Russia is today an exaggeration or malignant propaganda."[106] When Cardinal Theodor Innitzer pleaded for Western relief efforts for Ukrainians who were resorting to infanticide and cannibalism, the *Times* uncritically published the Soviet Union's chilling response: in the Soviet Union we have neither cannibals nor cardinals.[107]

George Orwell, whose novels *1984* and *Animal Farm* contained villains modeled after the Soviet leadership, chastised fellow Westerners for obscuring what the Soviets were doing. He specifically called out their use of ambiguous language, a tactic we now call *doublespeak* in reference to the deceptive *newspeak* language of *1984*. Orwell writes:

> Millions of peasants are robbed of their farms and sent trudging along the roads with no more than they can

SOCIALISM GETS A STATE

carry: this is called *transfer of population* or *rectification of frontiers*. People are imprisoned for years without trial, or shot in the back of the neck or sent to die of scurvy in Arctic lumber camps: this is called *elimination of unreliable elements*. Such phraseology is needed if one wants to name things without calling up mental pictures of them.[108]

It's no wonder Pope Pius XI grimly warned (one year before the *Holodomor*) about socialism "sinking" into Communism and how Communism seeks two objectives: unrelenting class warfare and absolute extermination of private ownership.

> Not secretly or by hidden methods does it do this, but publicly, openly, and by employing every and all means, even the most violent. To achieve these objectives there is nothing which it does not dare, nothing for which it has respect or reverence; and when it has come to power, it is incredible and portentlike in its cruelty and inhumanity (*Quadragesimo Anno* 112).

Pius XI also acknowledged the existence of a more moderate form of socialism that stood in contrast to authoritarian Communism. He noted how these systems were "opposing each other and even bitterly hostile" to one another. However, this conflict continued without either the tyrants or the moderates "abandoning a position fundamentally contrary to Christian truth that was characteristic of socialism" (111).

We will see why in the next chapter, as we take a closer look at Pope Pius XI's condemnation of all types of socialism.

IT'S IMPORTANT TO REMEMBER . . .

- Socialism was finally implemented politically on a national level beginning in 1918, when Lenin and his Bolsheviks emerged from the Russian Revolution at the head of the new U.S.S.R.

- The infamous Soviet "Five Year Plan" included the forced nationalization and state central planning of agriculture, resulting in a Ukrainian famine that killed millions.

- While sympathetic Western intellectuals and journalists downplayed the evils of Soviet policies, Pope Pius XI warned of Communism's inherent "cruelty and inhumanity."

10
PIUS XI AND SOCIALISM'S VICTIMS

In *Quadragesimo Anno*, Pope Pius XI reflected on themes Leo XIII put forward forty years before in *Rerum Novarum*, including the debate between capitalist and socialist economic systems. Like his predecessor, Pius XI had strong words for capitalists who hoarded wealth and treated workers as dispensable commodities on par with machines or sacks of coal. But he also said that capitalism "is not to be condemned in itself. And surely it is not of its own nature vicious" (101).

He went on to say that "when it comes to the present [capitalist] economic system, we have found it laboring under the gravest of evils." But whereas these evils could be remedied, the same was not true for socialism. Pius bluntly declared, "We have also summoned Communism and socialism again to judgment and have found all their forms, even the most modified, to wander far from the precepts of the gospel" (128).

THE SEDUCTIVE POISON OF SOCIALISM

Jose Mena, one of the authors of the socialist Tradinista! manifesto, claims, "The Church's condemnations of socialism tend to focus on other facets of left-wing political tradition: its thoroughgoing materialism and atheism, its hatred for God and for the natural family, and its totalitarian historical aspect."[109] He insists that the Catholic tradition still allows for a moderate socialism that orders private property to the common good through governmental oversight.

Yet, is it a coincidence that the major socialist states throughout history have always been atheistic or suppressed religious freedom? For Lenin said, "Marxism has always regarded all modern religions and churches, and each and every religious organization, as instruments of bourgeois reaction that serve to defend exploitation and to befuddle the working class."[110]

In order to complete their revolt against the upper class, their allies in religion had to be done away with as well. In 1922, the Soviet Union murdered twenty-eight Eastern Orthodox bishops and more than 1,200 priests.[111] A friend of Sergius I, the head of the Russian Orthodox Church, grimly recalled, "We [were like] chickens in a shed, from which the cook snatches out her victim in turn."[112] The much smaller Catholic Church fared no better, as by 1926 there were no Catholic bishops left in the country and by 1941 there were only two Catholic churches.[113]

Pius XI was aware of a socialism that "not only professes the rejection of violence but modifies and tempers to some degree, if it does not reject entirely, the class struggle and the abolition of private ownership" (*Quadragesimo Anno* 112). He commended the "just demands" of these socialists (such as stronger unions and worker protections), but said that their advocacy is unnecessary because there is "nothing in them now which is inconsistent with Christian truth, and much less are they special to socialism. Those who work solely toward such ends have, therefore, no reason to become socialists" (115).

Pius then spelled out the matter to Christians waiting "in suspense" to see if Christianity and socialism could ever be compatible with each other:

We make this pronouncement: Whether considered as a doctrine, or an historical fact, or a movement, socialism, if it remains truly socialism, even after it has yielded to truth and justice on the points which we have mentioned, cannot be reconciled with the teachings of the Catholic Church because its concept of society itself is utterly foreign to Christian truth (117).

Even if it doesn't reject the existence of God, or send dissenters to the gulags (forced labor camps), or terrorize the population with secret police, true socialism is not compatible with Christianity. One reason is that socialism rejects the Catholic principle of *subsidiarity*. This is the belief that a central, more central authority should subside or "sit back" and intervene only when lower, local authorities cannot address a problem. Pius formulated this principle, which "cannot be set aside or changed," this way:

Just as it is gravely wrong to take from individuals what they can accomplish by their own initiative and industry and give it to the community, so also it is an injustice and at the same time a grave evil and disturbance of right order to assign to a greater and higher association what lesser and subordinate organizations can do (79).

Although this principle wasn't formally articulated until the twentieth century, its precedents go all the way back to the Bible.

In the Old Testament, Moses' father-in-law Jethro warned him against using his leadership office to hear every dispute among the Israelites. "The thing is too heavy for you," he told Moses; "You are not able to perform it alone" (Exod. 18:18). Jethro then gave Moses this advice: "Choose able men from all the people, such as fear God, men who are trustworthy and who hate a bribe; and place such men over the people as rulers of thousands, of hundreds, of fifties, and of tens" (v. 21). In the New Testament, the apostles came to a similar conclusion when they felt overwhelmed by problems in local communities, and so they selected deacons to serve the people's needs (Acts 6:1–7).

Even Brianne Jacobs, in her defense of democratic socialism, admits that "[Catholic social teaching] has a clear warning about socialism" that is "related to the principle of subsidiarity, which states that individuals' needs should be met by local government or civil society whenever that is feasible."[114]

A big problem for socialism, be it radical or moderate, is that it says local authorities can't routinely provide for their own welfare and so a central authority (like the federal government) must do it for them. This rejection of subsidiarity is especially evident in socialism's scorn for the most fundamental local unit of authority in society: the family.

ABOLISH THE FAMILY?

In 1930—nearly co-incident with his economic encyclical and not for nothing—Pope Pius XI wrote an encyclical on Christian marriage and the family called *Casti Connubii* that upheld the Church's teaching on contraception when many people were justifying it in light of the Great Depression. But he also spoke of another sin against the family that seemed appealing to the economically disadvantaged: Communism.

He gives as one example, "the daily increasing corruption of morals and the unheard of degradation of the family in those lands where Communism reigns unchecked." Pius also cites *Arcanum Divniae,* Pope Leo XIII's encyclical on Christian marriage written fifty years earlier, which declared that "unless things change, the human family and state have every reason to fear lest they should suffer absolute ruin" (*Casti Connubii* 92).

Both popes repudiated the modern acceptance of divorce and warned how the destruction of the family leads to the destruction of the state because the family is the foundation of the state. But for socialists, a collective state could not exist without the destruction of the family. That's why *The Communist Manifesto* declares, "Abolition of the family! Even the most radical [men] flare up at this infamous proposal of the Communists."[115]

Engels argued in *The Origin of the Family, Private Property, and the State* that families bound together in matrimony were a modern invention created for the purpose of consolidating wealth. Wealth could only be redistributed, then, once the family unit was broken apart and dissolved into society. The early Soviet revolutionary Leon Trotsky said, "The revolution made a heroic effort to destroy the so-called 'family hearth'" and replace it with a "complete absorption of the housekeeping functions of the family by institutions of the socialist society."[116] This absorption included the indoctrination of children in government schools, or as Pope Pius XI described it:

There is a country where the children are actually being torn from the bosom of the family, to be formed (or, to speak more accurately, to be deformed and depraved) in godless schools and associations, to irreligion and hatred, according to the theories of advanced socialism; and thus is renewed in a real and more terrible manner the slaughter of the Innocents (*Divini Illius Magistri* 73).

Another early Soviet revolutionary, Alexandra Kollontai, said marriage would soon no longer be needed because, through "the collectivism of spirit" as she calls it, "the 'cold of inner loneliness' from which people in bourgeois culture have attempted to escape through love and marriage will disappear."[117]

It's no wonder that Pope Leo XIII denounced those who "think that the inherent character of marriage can be perverted with impunity; and who, disregarding the sanctity of religion and of the sacrament." He warned that both private families and public society risked being "miserably driven into that general confusion and overthrow of order which is even now the wicked aim of socialists and Communists" (*Arcanum* 32).

This assault on the family is not a bygone relic of Soviet Communism; it still appears in modern works based on Marx's philosophy—particular those that connect economic inequities with perceived cultural ones. One author in the popular anthology *Sisterhood Is Powerful* says that "we can't destroy the inequities between men and women until we destroy marriage."[118] Linda Gordon, writing in the journal *Women,* longs for the day when "families will be finally destroyed" after "a revolutionary social and economic organization permits people's needs for love and security to be met in ways that do not impose divisions of labor, or any external roles, at all."[119]

One way to see how Communism harms family structures is to consider its fanatical egalitarianism. Under this view, individual citizens owe the same loyalty and contribution to every man and woman in the state. This means that citizens who are parents owe no more to their children than they do to anyone else's. Preference for one's family—through, say, special sacrifice, or bequests, or gifts—have to be strictly forbidden because otherwise generous, caring families will cause some people to become unequal with others and create "class conflict."

But the family as instituted by God is not an egalitarian institution—the father has a different role from the son, and the daughter-in-law from the mother-in-law. The family is the classic example of unity arising from complementarity that we described in chapter eight. Since Communism wants none of that natural difference to play itself out in society, it must stamp out the family as the "cell" of society and as the first "school" of complementarity.

This can be seen in Sophie Anne Lewis's 2019 book *Full Surrogacy Now: Feminism Against Family*, which calls for the abolition of the family by promoting surrogates (people who gestate other women's children) as the primary means of reproduction for society. Her goal is to make it "normal for us to think about babies as made by many people. I would support policies that expand the number of people who are socially and legally recognized as central, fundamental players in the constitution of a person."[120]

THE INTRINSIC EVIL OF COMMUNISM

Although moderate socialism should be lauded for its rejection of class warfare, Pius XI points out that it still ends up either redundantly adopting the same ideals of Christian social teaching or else it "sinks into Communism." If it does that, then it is beyond any hope of salvaging because, as the pope wrote in *Divini Redemptoris*, "Communism is intrinsically wrong, and no one who would save Christian civilization may collaborate with it in any undertaking whatsoever" (58).

To say that something is *intrinsically* wrong means that it is wrong in and of itself, and thus is never permissible under any circumstances. War can *become* wrong if it is waged unjustly, but murder just *is* wrong because it is always wrong to directly kill an innocent person. Likewise, capitalism can *become* wrong if it allows evils like wage theft to take place, but it's not *always* wrong.

Communism, on the other hand, just *is* wrong by its very nature, because it violates a person's right to private property. Instead of respecting people's freedom to form families and associations for their good, socialists "hold that men are obliged, with respect to the producing of goods, to surrender and subject themselves entirely to society" (*Quadragesimo Anno* 119). Pius explains how this goal naturally leads to oppression:

> Indeed, possession of the greatest possible supply of things that serve the advantages of this life is considered of such great importance that the higher goods of man, liberty not excepted, must take a secondary place and even be sacrificed to the demands of the most efficient production of goods (119).

This inherent infringement of liberty can be seen in the common tactic of using secret police to maintain order in socialist states. Since socialism relies on central planning, it cannot tolerate the existence of any kind of market, including informal ones. In most countries, "black" markets deal with illegal products like drugs and weapons. But in a socialist country, the exchange of *any product* outside government venues constitutes an illegal black market that must be eliminated lest it disrupt the central planners' calculations.

In socialist East Germany, the *Stasi* (secret police) assigned one spy for every six citizens. Hundreds of thousands of part-time informers were also tasked with keeping tabs on the activities of their neighbors. According to John Koehler, a reporter who worked in both East and West Germany, "It would not have been unreasonable to assume that at least one Stasi informer was present in any party of ten or twelve dinner guests."[121]

Indeed, this same pattern of oppression and disrespect for human rights can be seen in the corpses socialism left behind as it swept the globe in the latter half of the twentieth century.

IT'S IMPORTANT TO REMEMBER . . .

- In *Quadragesimo Anno*, Pope Pius XI stressed that it was not merely on account of political repression that socialism was to be condemned, but because "its concept of society itself is utterly foreign to Christian truth."

- Socialism rejects the Catholic principle of *subsidiarity*, which says that government power should be exercised on the most local level possible.

- Just as socialism can have no private economic rivals to its control over the economy, it likewise naturally opposes the family (and its inherent "inequalities") as the basic unit of society.

11
SOCIALISM GOES GLOBAL

Mao Zedong's 1964 book of quotations (commonly called the "Little Red Book") is alleged to have sold nearly a billion copies worldwide, making it one of the best-selling books of all time. Along with its call for a "changeover from individual to socialist, collective ownership" it includes bits of wisdom like, "Political power grows out of the barrel of a gun."[122] This was certainly true for Mao after his Chinese communist party established itself as a powerful guerilla force whose membership grew from 100,000 in 1937 to 1.2 million in 1945.[123]

In 1949, Mao's forces defeated the Chinese nationalist party and the country was renamed the People's Republic of China. The nationalists fled to an island off the coast and formed the Republic of China, which is now called Taiwan. But whereas Taiwan's free-market policies helped it grow into an economic powerhouse over the next few decades, China's socialist policies led to one of the worst disasters in the history of humanity.

THE GREAT LEAP FORWARD

The country's new leader, now Chairman Mao, promised that all citizens would never have to worry about hunger because the Party would institute an "iron rice bowl" policy. Workers' jobs and wages would be guaranteed for life, with the expectation that worker productivity would increase because there would be no more worries about poverty. In reality, though, the absence of incentives and the necessity of turning all profits over to the government led workers and managers to become less and less productive.

The worst drop in production came in agriculture, where workers were prohibited from owning their own farms. Instead, farms were collectivized and all food production was turned over to the government. Most of the food was sold in order to support the plan for industrializing the country in accordance with a campaign dubbed the "Great Leap Forward." As with the Soviets before them, the government's mismanagement of food caused a famine. But the death toll from this famine dwarfed that of the *Holodomor*—the Soviet-caused Ukrainian famine in 1932–1933—to become the worst famine in the history of the world. According to Neil Hughes in his book *China's Economic Challenge*:

> The famine that followed in the wake of the Great Leap Forward claimed 30 million lives. Children especially suffered, as reflected in mortality data showing the median age at death, which fell from 17.6 years of age in 1957 to 9.7 years of age in 1963. One-half of the people dying in China were under ten years old.[124]

Yang Jisheng was once a member of the Communist Party but left after its brutal killing of hundreds of peaceful protesters in Tiananmen Square in 1989. He then wrote the most in-depth history of the Chinese famine ever published, called *Tombstone: the Great Chinese Famine, 1958–1962*. He explains the book's title by saying that he sought to erect three tombstones: "for my father, who died of starvation in 1959 . . . for the 36 million Chinese who died of starvation, and . . . for the system that brought about the Great Famine."[125]

The book includes grotesque details of corpses being kept in beds in order to trick government officials into thinking they were alive so that relatives could receive their food rations.[126] Cannibalism was common; children who ate their own parents admitted "the heels and palms tasted the best."[127] A government official who opened a granary for starving peasants later committed suicide in response to what other officials considered to be an act of treason. Jisheng says, "No matter how loud the peasants' laments of starvation, those in the top leadership regarded them as the cries of opposition to socialism."[128]

And, like Walter Duranty before them, Western intellectuals denied the existence of the famine and praised Mao as a revolutionary figure who fought for the poor.

The feminist philosopher Simone de Beauvoir said in 1958 that "life in China today is exceptionally pleasant." American journalist Hans Koning, writing in 1966, said China was "almost as painstakingly careful about human lives as New Zealand." Also in 1966, Mao launched the "Cultural Revolution" that sought to purge capitalist influences in the country. An estimated one million people were killed; Mao bragged that the first Chinese emperor "only buried alive 460 scholars, while we buried 46,000."[129]

THE DARKNESS OF NORTH KOREA

Defenses of socialist China still pop up today, as is evident in British socialist Jeremy Corbyn's claim that "the present prosperity in China is based upon a collective economy and not on an individual and market oriented economy." But this is false: China's economic growth did not begin to catch up to Hong Kong's and Taiwan's until after it adopted a limited market-based economy beginning in 1980. The anthology *Reforming Asian Socialism: the Growth of Market Institutions* shows that almost all socialist countries in Asia have embraced some form of capitalism in order to avoid economic stagnation. There is only one notable exception: the Democratic People's Republic of Korea—or North Korea.

After World War II, the Korean peninsula ceased to be under Japanese control and was divided between the pro-American Republic of Korea (South Korea) and the Communist, Soviet-backed Democratic People's Republic of Korea (North Korea). Both nations fought for control of the peninsula during the Korean War, which ended with an armistice in 1953 and both countries are divided by a heavily guarded "demilitarized zone" to the present day. North Korea adopted the principle of *Juche*, or self-reliance, developed by their first leader Kim Il-Sung. The North Korean leaders believed their superior lifestyle and production numbers would encourage a worker's revolution in South Korea and finally reunite both countries. Fast-forward six decades and a single nighttime satellite image proves this kind of thinking is delusional.

When viewed from space, South Korea twinkles like any modern, vibrant country at night whereas North Korea is almost entirely dark. Ninety-seven percent of North Korea's roads are unpaved and, outside the capital of Pyongyang, some of the best-looking homes are in a fake "Peace Village" that has no residents and was built along the border solely to impress (and possibly attract immigrants from) the south.[130]

The two Koreas weren't always this unequal, however. In 1960, both countries had a gross domestic product of about $5 billion. Today, North Korea's GDP is barely at $20 billion whereas South Korea has surpassed $1.5 trillion, making it the fourth-largest economy in Asia. This difference in wealth is starkly evident not only in satellite photos—thanks to better access to food and medicine, South Korea's people average about two inches taller than their northern counterparts.[131] One researcher concludes, "North Korean performance faltered due to its inward-looking policies . . . [it] remains a poor country with low growth and a generally isolationist communist party."[132]

But this doesn't stop Western intellectuals like the World Health Organization's Margaret Chan from acting like fools in their stubborn defense of anything socialist. Because it's a crime to leave North Korea, the population has a relatively high percentage of doctors, something Chan says "most other developing countries would envy." She also spins the people's undernourishment as a good thing: unlike in other Asian countries, North Koreans don't suffer from obesity![133]

Well, that's one way to describe the effects of food shortages and the occasional famine that results from communal food production.

FAULTY LIBERATION THEOLOGY

While socialism was mixing with Korean and Chinese philosophy in East Asia, in the Western Hemisphere, particularly in Central and South America, it became tragically intertwined with Catholicism through *liberation theology.*

As Trent notes in *Counterfeit Christs*, one of liberation theology's key ideas is the Marxist principle of "class struggle," or the claim that the upper classes always cause others to be poor and so the lower classes must seize political power and establish their own "dictatorship" with the goal of creating a "classless society." In Gustavo Gutierrez's classic text *A Theology of Liberation,* he writes, "The class struggle is a fact that Christians cannot dodge and in the face of which the demands of the gospel must be clearly stated."[134]

In 1984, the Congregation for the Doctrine of the Faith (CDF) released its *Instruction on Certain Aspects of the "Theology of Liberation."* The CDF agreed that Christians have a special obligation to help the poor (sometimes called the "preferential option for the poor") and should not tolerate unjust conditions that create widespread poverty. But it also noted that liberation theology errs when it locates the source of evil in class conflict instead of in man's inherent tendency to sin because of our fallen nature.[135]

In his encyclical *Spe Salvi*, Pope Benedict XVI similarly criticized Marxism, saying that man "is not merely the product of economic conditions, and it is not possible to redeem him purely from the outside by creating a favorable economic environment" (21). The CDF also warned about the consequences that can result from trying to join theology with something as contrary to the Faith as Marxism. It quoted Pope Paul VI, who said it was "dangerous" to "enter into the practice of class struggle and of its Marxist interpretation while failing to see the kind of totalitarian society to which this process slowly leads."[136]

In fact, by opposing the conditions for a thriving business economy, liberation theologians and their political allies have wrought nothing but harm for the poor that they profess to champion.

COMMUNISM IN CUBA

A prime example of this kind of society is Communist Cuba, which formed after Fidel Castro's revolution in 1959 and has since seen the execution of more than 10,000 people.[137] One of Castro's most important allies was Ernesto "Che" Guevara, a young revolutionary whose steely gaze can be found on posters and T-shirts at colleges across the country. The many students who lionize Che as a "rebel" apparently don't know that he banned newspapers and executed people even if he wasn't sure they were guilty of anything.[138] The new Communist government, like every other one before and after it, also imprisoned dissidents into forced labor camps—in this case with the absurd euphemism of "Military Units to Aid Production."[139]

Like every other socialist regime, Cuba's policy of collective food production led to food shortages and required the government to issue "ration tickets" for citizens to redeem in small quantities. Yes, U.S. trade embargoes hampered the economy, but they don't explain why Cuba experienced shortages in its own domestically produced goods (especially during the Cold War when Soviet funds offset the impact of U.S. embargoes). In Eliana Cardsos and Ann Helwege's book *Cuba After Communism,* the authors explain that under the state's socialist policies,

> Cubans cannot easily set up a small business on the side. People say there are hairdresser and seamstresses, but few hang up a sign for services. A broken pipe meant waiting a few weeks for the state plumber to arrive. Access to most goods is too limited and the penalties too high for people to set up illegal shops and kiosks. The state not only fails to provide goods but prohibits people from filling the gap with informal markets.[140]

Even as recently as 2019, Cubans were reporting long lines at grocery stores to buy basic food items like eggs and chicken. One report noted that "Cuba imports 60 to 70 percent of its food. A handful of agricultural reforms in recent years have failed to boost output in its inefficient, centrally planned economy."[141] People who try to circumvent these inefficiencies through black market sales of things like eggs or meat can be imprisoned for up to twenty years.[142]

Despite the state's harsh penalties, illegal markets supply people with most of their needs through networks of *socios*:

citizens who steal goods that can't be bought in normal markets and then trade with one another for basic goods. Katherine Hirschfield, who spent nine months in Cuba for her dissertation research, described how one man would steal towels from his hotel for his *socio*, who then repays him with beer he steals from his factory. The first man, according to one of Hirschfield's sources, "will then trade the beer to the maid for a supply of soap, which he'll either give to his [suppliers] or sell on the black market. Everybody does it. It's the only way to survive."[143]

Some socialists denounce Cuba's violent past but tout its modern achievements such as its allegedly high life expectancies and low infant mortality rates. They say this disproves the idea that socialism is detrimental to the common good. But a 2018 study in the *Journal of Health and Policy Planning* paints a darker picture.

It says that health care workers, under pressure to meet government quotas, alter data, and even pressure women to have abortions. The authors reveal how "physicians likely reclassified early neonatal deaths as late fetal deaths, thus deflating the infant mortality statistics and propping up life expectancy. . . . If we combine the misreporting of late fetal deaths and pressured abortions, life expectancy would drop by between 1.46 and 1.79 years for men."[144]

As a result of these repressive policies, over a million Cubans have fled the country in makeshift boats to the United States. During the 1960s the number of unaccompanied minors became so great that the Catholic Welfare Bureau launched "Operation Pedro Pan" to provide housing and resources for children whose parents could not join them in their flight from Castro's communist regime.[145] Even in 2019, Cuba ranked sixth among countries whose citizens were fleeing to the United States with "credible fear" asylum claims.[146]

And, as we'll see, this constant human desire to flee socialism is what led to the demise of the largest socialist country in the history of the world.

IT'S IMPORTANT TO REMEMBER . . .

- China's adoption of socialism following a civil war led to the same economic and agricultural failures—and similar deadly famines—that Russia experienced.

- Socialism in North Korea has made it a literal and figurative dark spot in what is otherwise an economically bustling East Asia.

- In South America and the Caribbean, socialism has likewise produced predictable poverty and human misery. In some places it gets mixed up with Catholic teaching into something called *liberation theology*.

12
MODERN POPES VS. MODERN SOCIALISM

Soviet first secretary Nikita Khrushchev was not one for subtlety. During a 1960 meeting at the U.N. General Assembly, Khrushchev became enraged when a delegate from the Philippines spoke of "the peoples of Eastern Europe and elsewhere which have been deprived of the free exercise of their civil and political rights and which have been swallowed up, so to speak, by the Soviet Union."[147] In response, Khrushchev banged his shoe on a table in order to disrupt the delegate and get his own turn to speak.[148]

Some people think the shoe-banging incident was also when Khrushchev told the U.S., "We will bury you," but that actually happened four years earlier at a gathering of Western ambassadors. He said, "About the capitalist states, it doesn't depend on you whether or not we exist. If you don't like us, don't accept our invitations, and don't invite us to come to see you. Whether you like it or not, history is on our side. We will bury you!"[149]

Khrushchev later claimed that he meant the Soviet Union would outlive capitalist states that would eventually succumb to workers' revolutions. And as the twentieth century progressed there were worker revolutions—but they consisted of workers who overthrew *Communist* chains as Western nations and the Catholic Church faithfully stood by them.

SOCIALISM IN GERMANY

In 1961, Pope St. John XXIII published the encyclical *Mater et Magistra,* which continued the denunciation of socialism made under Leo XIII and Pius XI. He affirmed that private property has its origin in natural law and that paying wages to workers is not unjust in itself but only becomes unjust under certain conditions that must be avoided. Echoing Pius XI before him, he wrote, "Justice demands that account be taken not only of the needs of the individual workers and their families, but also of the financial state of the business concern for which they work and of 'the economic welfare of the whole people" (*Mater et Magistra* 33). The pope then turned his attention to socialism:

> Pope Pius XI further emphasized the fundamental op-
> position between Communism and Christianity, and
> made it clear that no Catholic could subscribe even
> to moderate socialism. The reason is that socialism
> is founded on a doctrine of human society which is
> bounded by time and takes no account of any objective
> other than that of material well-being. Since, therefore,
> it proposes a form of social organization which aims
> solely at production, it places too severe a restraint on
> human liberty, at the same time flouting the true no-
> tion of social authority (34).

Three months after *Mater et Magistra* was published, the Soviets unveiled their newest "restraint on human liberty" in the form of the Berlin Wall, which was part of the larger, post-war division of the country. East Germany became a Soviet-occupied "workers' state" while West Germany became an independent country that functioned under a capitalist economy. Like North and South Korea, East and West Germany became perfect "laboratories" to test socialism's economic merits. Before World War II, the eastern part of Germany had a higher per-capita income than the west, but post-war socialist policies turned East Germany into a drab, run-down country that Indian economist B.R. Shenoy likened to "a prison camp."[150]

During the 1950s, what had been 50 percent marginal tax rates for income over $600 (recall that the Third Reich was a "national socialist" regime) were changed in the West only to apply to people who made more than $42,000 a year. The ensuing growth of efficient industries led to the *Wirtschaftswunder*—an "economic miracle" of growth and prosperity—while East Germany's economy remained stagnant and unproductive.[151] To provide one example: by the 1980s, the West German automotive industry had become a global engineering force whereas East German companies were still mass-producing outdated cars like the infamous Trabant, which lacked basic amenities like a fuel gauge and rear seat belts and required drivers to pre-mix gas and oil for its ancient two-stroke engine.[152]

Shenoy concludes:

The contrast in prosperity is convincing proof of the superiority of the forces of freedom over centralized planning. It is difficult to resist the inference that workers in East Berlin, deprived of the incentives of full property rights over the fruits of one's effort, are loath to put in their best.[153]

So many Germans fled the country that a 1955 East German propaganda tract described this behavior as "an act of political and moral backwardness" for which "workers throughout Germany will demand punishment."[154] When threats and propaganda failed to stem the exodus, travel was legally prohibited and, overnight, an 87-mile-long wall was erected to isolate West-controlled zones in the capital of Berlin. The wall included barbed wire, 116 guard towers, and "dead zones" in front of the wall that made it easier to find and shoot would-be defectors.

Socialists may fantasize about workers leaving capitalist countries for socialist ones, but in the real world, people who want to provide their children with basic necessities and a hopeful future choose capitalism over socialism every time. The proof of this can be seen in the contrast between capitalist countries that use barriers to keep people from illegally *entering* and socialist countries (like East Germany and North Korea) that use barriers to keep people from illegally *escaping.*

BACK IN THE U.S.S.R.

In 1971, Pope Paul VI lamented about Christians being deceived into supporting an unrealistic socialism over sound Catholic social doctrine. He wrote, "Too often Christians attracted by socialism tend to idealize it in terms which, apart from anything else, are very general: a will for justice, solidarity, and equality" (*Octogesima Adveniens* 31). He pointed out that support for the dignity of workers and human rights is properly found in Christian moral teaching. An example of this during the Cold War was Poland's Solidarity movement.

In the 1980s, Polish workers formed the first non-state-controlled trade union in a Communist country and called it *Solidarity*. It used non-violent tactics to oppose Communist oppression of workers and received significant support from the Catholic Church. For example, when Communists imposed martial law in order to disrupt union activity, Catholic Masses became one of the few safe places for people to gather in public.

This wasn't just for political show: many members of Solidarity were devout Catholics who kept pictures of the Blessed Virgin at their factory work posts. One outspoken priest, Fr. Jerzy Popiełuszko, not only offered Mass but explicitly preached against the government's socialist policies. He knew such actions were dangerous but considered them better than doing nothing in the face of evil:

> To preserve one's dignity as man is to remain interiorly free even in external slavery, to remain oneself in all situations of life, to remain in the truth, even if that is to cost us dearly. Because it costs a lot to speak the truth. Only the weeds, in other words, petty, mediocre things, are cheap. But for the wheat of truth, as with all great and beautiful things, one must pay the demanding price of self-sacrifice.[155]

Fr. Popiełuszko finally paid this price on October 19, 1984 when three members of the country's security service kidnapped him, beat him to death, and dumped his body into a reservoir. He was thirty-seven.

But far from crushing the movement, Popiełuszko's death galvanized Solidarity, and the Church has declared him a beatified martyr.

For the previous forty years, the Soviet Union had subsidized its satellite states' failing economies, but falling oil prices in the mid-eighties forced Soviet premier Mikhail

Gorbachev to cut off economic aid.[156] This loosened the U.S.S.R.'s grip, and Solidarity members were now able to fight for Poland's freedom. As a result, in 1989, Solidarity's leader, Lech Walesa, was elected president of Poland in the country's first free election in decades.

As other former Communist states renounced their ties to the Soviet Union, the dismantling of old Soviet borders caused a surge of East German citizens to bypass the wall and enter West Germany. The flood of refugees leaving East Germany became so difficult to manage that the government authorized limited, round-trip travel directly through the Berlin Wall. On November 9, 1989, East German spokesman Gunter Schabowski made a media appearance to announce the plan—but hadn't been told all the details about the regulations.

When asked when the plans would go into effect, he said, "As far as I know . . . a decision has been made . . . to issue a regulation that will make it possible for every citizen . . . to emigrate." When German reporter Peter Brinkmann asked Schabowski, "When does that go into force?" the Communist party leader scanned his unfamiliar notes and simply blurted out, "Right away."[157] This gaffe motivated thousands of East Germans to test out their newfound freedom and overwhelm the wall's security checkpoints. The crowds were eventually allowed to pass without any restrictions and, later that night, exuberant people young and old to begin to demolish the Berlin Wall.

COMMUNIST FAILURES, CAPITALIST WARNINGS

In May 1991, two years after the fall of the Berlin Wall but four months before the Soviet Union officially dissolved, Pope John Paul II wrote an encyclical called *Centesimus Annus*, or "one hundred years later" in honor of Pope Leo

XIII's publication of *Rerum Novarum*. He said, "By defining the nature of the socialism of his day as the suppression of private property, Leo XIII arrived at the crux of the problem" (*Centesimus Annus* 12). He then says "the Marxist solution has failed" because:

> A person who is deprived of something he can call "his own," and of the possibility of earning a living through his own initiative, comes to depend on the social machine and on those who control it. This makes it much more difficult for him to recognize his dignity as a person, and hinders progress toward the building up of an authentic human community (13).

The fall of Communism did not mean that the answers to man's economic problems were now abundantly clear. It "certainly removes an obstacle to facing these problems," he wrote, but he also made it clear that the problems of poverty and corruption still remained. Some might have said that capitalism could now take over and address those problems, but the Church took a more nuanced approach. The pope even warned of a radical capitalistic ideology that "blindly entrusts their solution to the free development of market forces" (42).

As we'll see, this does not mean that capitalism is an opposing evil to socialism. Instead, it means that any science that aims to increase human well-being, be it medicine, politics, or economics, must be guided by sound principles ordered toward our ultimate well-being as human beings made in the image of God.

IT'S IMPORTANT TO REMEMBER . . .

- In the second half of the twentieth century, the Church continued its consistent denunciation of socialism.

- Socialism in East Germany led not only to decades of economic and cultural stagnation, but to a wall with barbed wire keeping its people from escaping to the West.

- Popular movements in Soviet satellite states, particularly in Poland where the papacy of John Paul II was a rallying point, worked for increased economic and personal freedom until the eventual collapse of the Soviet Union.

PART FOUR

IS CAPITALISM
THE ANSWER?

13
CAPITALISM AND HUMAN NATURE

In the 1987 film *Wall Street,* cutthroat businessman Gordon Gekko lectures the members of a shareholder's meeting. "Greed," he tells them, "is good. Greed is right. Greed works."

For many people since, Gekko became the embodiment of the greedy, selfish capitalist who elevates profits over people. One author says, "Capitalism takes the position that 'greed is good,' which its supporters say is a positive thing—greed drives profits and profits drive innovation and product development, which means there are more choices available for those who can afford them."[158]

Are critics right? Is capitalism an evil economic system that Catholics can't support because it relies on the sin of greed?

FROM WANTS TO CREATION

If you ask people what fundamental values drive capitalism, they might indeed talk about greed, profits, or selfishness. That's understandable if their only reference point for capitalism is a character like Gordon Gekko or an Ayn Rand book like *The Virtue of Selfishness.* But the fundamental values that drive capitalism are actually good ones: freedom and creativity.

In a free market, no one can force you to buy what a business is selling; the business has to persuade you to enter freely into a mutually beneficial exchange. When I buy a donut for a dollar, it's because, at that moment, I value the donut more than the dollar and the baker values the dollar more than the donut. In that sense, capitalism can be summarized as: *Give me what I want and I will give you what you want.* (In contrast, we might summarizes socialism as: *Give the state what you have and it will give you what it thinks you need.*)

Obviously, this isn't a profound altruism like, "Give to those in need regardless of what you want," but capitalism isn't meant to be a profound moral system. Capitalism is a tool, based on discovery of the nature of things, that in spite of its weaknesses encourages people to channel their natural self-interest in a way that indirectly brings about good for others.

Capitalism also flows from our natural human creativity. When you see any ten-year-old boy with Lego bricks you see the natural human desire to wonder, "What can I make" followed by the will to take an idea and "make it real." Animals don't create new or better tools and, as Adam Smith pointed out, they don't make deals or exchanges. But human beings have an innate desire to create and exchange their creations with one another, and this benefits humanity as a whole even if some people may use it to cause harm.

Sure, some people will create frivolous goods that don't really benefit anyone. The world today doesn't mourn the disappearance of past fads like pet rocks! But most entrepreneurs will create useful things or improve existing goods to make them more beneficial to the world, and some will create things we couldn't imagine living without—like cars or computers. In all these cases, capitalism is a force for good.

Yes, some will create sinful goods and services the world would be better off without, like pornography or prostitution. But as an economic tool, capitalism shouldn't be blamed when it's used to serve sinful desires any more than other tools (like kitchen knives) are blamed when they're used for evil ends (like stabbing innocent people).

To make an even better analogy, dating (or what we could call "romantic markets") can be opportunities for people merely to satisfy their lusts and engage in fornication. But that wouldn't justify forbidding free, romantic interactions and having government central planners arrange everyone's marriages. Such a solution would create more evils than it tries to solve, and of course it would do nothing to reduce sins of lust. In the same way, forbidding commercial markets in favor of centrally allocating goods only creates greater evils, and in the end does not eliminate the tendency toward greed that is part of our fallen nature.

Some critics say that we are only selfish because capitalism, with its emphasis on satisfying endless wants, *makes us that way.* They say that if we adopted socialism we could restore the primitive altruism our ancestors practiced before we were inundated with a consumerist culture that brainwashed us into thinking we need "stuff" to be happy. But this view ignores thousands of years of history that lacked capitalism but still had lots of avarice—and with it, violent crime. The cognitive scientist Steven Pinker argues that we live in the least criminal and war-torn age in all of human history, and capitalism helped bring this about, because "when it's cheaper to buy things than to steal them, people don't steal them."[159]

This tendency for free markets to curb our base impulses is summarized in Adam Smith's example of an "invisible hand" that guides producers in the market to benefit others "in spite of their natural selfishness and rapacity."[160] Capitalism doesn't *require* greed; it *restrains* it through voluntary, mutual exchange. In his book *Money, Greed, and God,* Jay Richards explains:

Even if the butcher is selfish, even if the butcher would love nothing more than to sell you a spoiled chunk of grisly beef in exchange for your worldly goods and leave you homeless, the butcher can't make you buy his meat in a free economy. He has to offer you meat you'll freely buy. The cruel, greedy butcher, in other words, has to look for ways to set up win–win scenarios. Even to satisfy his greed, he has to meet your desires. The market makes this happen. That's making the best of a bad situation, and of a bad butcher.[161]

We must remember that greed and selfishness are not strictly the same as *self-interest*, which is a good inclination God instilled within us. The conflation of a good, healthy type of self-interest with mere greed or selfishness contributes to a great deal of confusion about economies built on free exchanges.

Jesus said that we should love our neighbor as ourselves, not that we should love our neighbor *instead* of ourselves. There is a proper kind of self-love, rooted in humility, that moves us to care for our own animal and spiritual needs in a manner befitting a son or daughter of God. We ordinarily meet our own needs before we meet the needs of others, which is good because if we didn't meet our basic needs we wouldn't be much help to others for long.

It's the same reason that airplane attendants instruct us to secure our own oxygen masks before those of children next to us. St. Thomas Aquinas put it this way, "man's love for himself is the model of his love for another. But the model exceeds the copy. Therefore, out of charity, a man ought to love himself more than his neighbor."[162]

THE "P" WORD

In *Letters to a Young Evangelical,* Christian author Tony Campolo complains that the typical good produced in a capitalist system "doesn't meet anybody's needs, but is simply designed to generate profits."[163] Yet profit is not the same thing as "money" nor is it something that only exists for greedy people to hoard.

Profit is a sign that a business *is* meeting people's needs by providing them with something they want at a price that is higher than the cost of producing it. It's an indicator of a healthy business, which is a business poised to grow and thus benefit more people with the good or service.

When critics of capitalism quip about how the system "values profits over people" they forget that profitable businesses *show that people are being benefited.* Workers are getting paid and consumers are getting what they want, and not just the "well off" ones. The economist Joseph Schumpeter says, "The capitalist achievement does not typically consist in providing more silk stockings for queens but in bringing them within reach of factory girls in return for steadily decreasing amounts of effort."[164]

Instead of measuring business success with profits, socialist economies measure it with output. Industries that produce the most goods (irrespective of whether people actually want them) are considered the most important and, as a result, are given the biggest budgets by the state. This means socialist businesses do whatever they can to increase their budgets, even if that means not meeting consumer needs. When a business in the free market fails to meet people's needs, it loses profits and either adapts or closes. But when industries under socialism (or even some public-sector businesses in market economies) fail to meet people's needs, they can operate indefinitely as long as the state subsidizes them.[165]

It's also a fallacy to compare real-world capitalism, with its admitted fair share of greedy, unscrupulous entrepreneurs, to an idealized socialism that never has and never can exist because of our fallen human nature. In the real world, socialism reaps a "harvest of misery" because it expects people to act in ways that are contrary to their fallen human nature. Remember what happened when the pilgrims expected everyone to act only for the interest of others? They quickly used that as an excuse to do whatever they could to benefit themselves, and this almost led to their ruin.

That capitalism is not essentially built upon greed is evident in the fact that even if people weren't greedy they would still be *needy*—and free markets allow people to exchange goods and services in order to meet their needs. In fact, capitalism allows people to accumulate so much wealth that they are capable of engaging in acts of altruism to a degree previously unknown in human history.

A GENEROSITY OPPORTUNITY

In 2012, Bruce Springsteen began his "Wrecking Ball Tour" throughout Europe, dedicating songs to those experiencing economic hardship. One song described "greedy thieves and robber barons" who "destroyed our families, factories and they took our homes." But although it makes for doleful lyrics, the idea that capitalists are just a bunch of "robber barons" who get rich at the expense of the poor is a myth.

The term "robber baron" comes from the medieval German *raubritter* or "robber knights" who charged illegal tolls on public rivers and roads.[166] But whereas these thieves use force to steal money from poor people who were just using public goods that actually belonged to them, modern capitalists like Cornelius Vanderbilt and John D. Rockefeller helped create massive amounts of wealth by providing, among other things, better ways to traverse public roads and rivers.[167]

Rockefeller has been called the richest man who ever lived, and he got that way in the late nineteenth century because his company, Standard Oil, made affordable kerosene that everybody wanted. He said, "Let the good work go on. We must ever remember we are refining oil for the poor man and he must have it cheap and good."[168] Even the poorest of Americans could now have reliable heating and lamp oil, and the byproducts of kerosene were used to create cheap gasoline for the newly invented automobile.

Rockefeller became the world's first billionaire and he gave away half his fortune (worth $10 billion today) to charity. His philanthropy included founding a black women's college and a medical foundation that later eradicated hookworm.[169] That's why it's painfully ironic to hear a socialist like Che Guevara complain about the "poverty and suffering required for a Rockefeller to emerge" given the violence and suffering that was required for someone like Guevara to emerge as a socialist icon.[170]

The generosity of someone like Rockefeller is not an anomaly. The Charities Aid Foundation has shown the nations that provide the most help to strangers are those that have the freest economies. The five most "individualistic" countries in the survey (United States, Australia, New Zealand, Canada, and the United Kingdom) ranked second, third, fourth, sixth, and eighth respectively when it comes to having generous citizens. In contrast, those few countries that bucked the global trend toward individualism included some with the lowest socioeconomic development, including Armenia, Malaysia, Mali, and Uruguay.[171]

Just to be clear, we are not saying that capitalism by itself creates a just world and makes everyone charitable and morally upright. Capitalism is a tool—discovered in nature—that facilitates the exchange of goods and services, and like any tool it can be abused. For example, some of the "robber barons" of the early twentieth century did increase their wealth through unethical business practices, such as insider trading. But *abusus non usum tollit*: abuse does not take away the proper use, and this will become clear when we examine what the Church has to say about capitalism.

IT'S IMPORTANT TO REMEMBER . . .

- Capitalism is not really based on greed but on *self-interest*, which is a natural human instinct that can be channeled to good ends.

- Profit is a natural marker for economic success; and although it can be acquired immorally and used viciously, it's also necessary for the creation of wealth, the alleviation of poverty, and the practice of philanthropy.

14

THE CHURCH ON CAPITALISM

Throughout history, the Church has often used heresy as an opportunity to define and clarify the true teachings of the Faith. When Arians attacked the divinity of Christ in the third century, the Church taught correct Christology at the first ecumenical councils. When heretics branded the Eucharist a mere symbol in the eleventh century, the Fourth Lateran Council reaffirmed Christ's real presence in the sacrament.

In the nineteenth century, socialism became the "founding heresy" that spurred the development of *Catholic social doctrine*. It provided an opportunity to teach "principles of right order" regarding social, political, and economic questions. *Quadragesimo Anno* takes up the issue of capitalism because "its most bitter accuser, socialism" had made serious arguments against it and, in doing so, the encyclical answers the question: "If a Catholic can't be a socialist, can he be a capitalist?" (98).

ANSWERING A "BITTER ACCUSER"

Pius XI's goal in *Quadragesimo Anno* was to answer the "social question," or the question of what should be done about the growing strife and inequality between the small class of people who owned property like factories and the larger class of people who worked for them. Although the discussion mentions other economic systems that can lead to "miserable and wretched condition[s]," Pius's main focus was on capitalism, which he defined as "that economic system, wherein, generally, some provide capital while others provide labor for a joint economic activity" (100).

We must point out that the debate over capitalism is not about whether we should have "laissez-faire" capitalism instead of state-regulated capitalism. Since capitalism can only exist when the government enforces private property rights and recognizes contractual agreements, it's impossible to leave the state out of it entirely. The question is, rather, "*How* should the state view and intervene in the affairs of free market economies?" To that question, Pius offered two conclusions.

First, he said, the state should not treat capitalism as something intrinsically evil; this economic system "is not to be condemned in itself" (101). Second, following Leo XIII, the state should make sure free markets adhere to "norms of right order" by correcting violations of these norms. These include conditions that "scorn the human dignity of the workers, the social character of economic activity and social justice itself, and the common good" (101). The state could, for example, require factory owners to implement commonsense safety measures to protect workers from occupational hazards.

But nowhere did Pius XI say that *socialism* could be acceptable provided it adhered to certain moral norms. He admitted that, "like all errors," socialism "contains some truth" (120). But the truths of socialism (which are shared by Christianity, thus making them not strictly socialist in nature) are not enough to redeem a system that, he continues, "is based nevertheless on a theory of human society peculiar to itself and irreconcilable with true Christianity."

And so, whereas there can be Christian capitalists who use their wealth to better the world, according to Pius, "Religious socialism, Christian socialism, are contradictory terms; no one can be at the same time a good Catholic and a true socialist."[172]

POPE FRANCIS ON CAPITALISM

Being critical of capitalism doesn't mean you are an anti-capitalist. Adam Smith, the father of modern economic thought, warned about capitalism's vices. For example, he noted how the ability to freely set prices can lead businessmen into "a conspiracy against the public, or in some contrivance to raise prices."[173] But Smith recognized that capitalism is a worthwhile system because it works *despite* human imperfections. Socialism, on the other hand, requires everyone always to be perfectly altruistic, and that's why it always fails.

So when Pope Francis says that under capitalism "people can easily get caught up in a whirlwind of needless buying and spending" (*Laudato Si* 203), he's absolutely right. Markets may be able to provide lots of things to buy, but that doesn't mean we should try to find meaning and happiness in those things. The pope also said that "once greed for money presides over the entire socioeconomic system, it ruins society." But, as we saw in the last chapter, greed is a property of morally defective capitalists—it is not intrinsic to capitalism in the same way that confiscation and redistribution are intrinsic to socialism.[174] William F. Buckley put it well: "The trouble with socialism is *socialism*. The trouble with capitalism is *capitalists*."[175]

When the pope visited the United States in 2016, he even gave an address to Congress where he affirmed that capitalism could be a good thing when it is properly ordered toward the good. He commended the U.S.'s efforts to fight poverty and said that "part of this great effort is the creation and distribution of wealth." He went on:

> The right use of natural resources, the proper application of technology and the harnessing of the spirit of enterprise are essential elements of an economy which seeks to be modern, inclusive, and sustainable. "Business is a noble vocation directed to producing wealth and improving the world. It can be a fruitful source of prosperity for the area in which it operates, especially if it sees the creation of jobs as an essential part of its service to the common good"[176] (*Laudato Si* 129).

Pope Francis's former mentor, Fr. Juan Carlos Scannone, says the pontiff "doesn't criticize market economics, but rather the fetishization of money and the free market."[177] When critics labeled Francis a Marxist for his criticism of "trickle-down" economics, the pope said in response that "Marxist ideology is wrong."[178] In fact, Pope Francis's dual criticisms of capitalism and socialism echo the writings of John Paul II.

THE CHURCH AND ECONOMICS

In *Centesimus Annus,* John Paul II said that profit has a "legitimate role" in the function of a business but that it's not the *only* indicator that a business is doing well. The human dignity of workers matters too, and if capitalism is left unchecked it can become "ruthless" and leads to "inhuman exploitation" (33). But despite his criticisms, the pope never said that this system is intrinsically evil like socialism, nor does he offer an alternative economic system in its place. In fact, John Paul reaffirms the teaching of previous popes who said that the Church not only does not offer the world a "Catholic" system of economics, it *can't* offer such a system.

The Church's authority relates to teaching about faith and morals; but economics is a science that studies the production, distribution, and consumption of goods and services. As Nobel economist James Buchanan put it, economics studies "the ordinary business of man making his living."[179] Economics can answer questions like, "What gives rise to the wealth of nations?" but not moral questions like, "How should I make use of my wealth?" The Church can offer moral and theological principles to guide secular disciplines, but it can't replace those disciplines.

To make an analogy, the Church offers principles to doctors to guide them in practicing medicine morally. Some of these values have their roots in classical wisdom, like the Hippocratic Oath's condemnation of abortion and assisted suicide, and some in teachings stemming from divine revelation. But the Church doesn't tell doctors how to create health in their medical interventions. Only the science of medicine can tell us how to restore a person's health when he becomes sick.

Likewise, the Church offers principles to economists to guide them in moral application of economics, but it doesn't dictate a "Catholic" way to create wealth. That's the job of those competent in the science of economics. That's why Pope Pius XI taught that "economics and moral science each employs its own principles in its own sphere" (*Quadragesimo Anno* 42). He said God entrusted the Church with exercising its authority "not of course in matters of technique for which she is neither suitably equipped nor endowed by office, but in all things that are connected with the moral law" (41).

JOHN PAUL II ON CAPITALISM

Since economics is not a field related to theology or the moral law, John Paul II made it clear that "the Church has no models to present." Instead, economic models "that are real and truly effective can only arise within the framework of different historical situations, through the efforts of all those who responsibly confront concrete problems in all their social, economic, political, and cultural aspects." The Church does have, however, a role to play in offering guidance on economic questions that overlap with moral and social doctrine. "For such a task," he says, "the Church offers her social teaching as an *indispensable and ideal orientation*" (*Centesimus Annus* 43).

In that respect, in *Centesimus Annus* John Paul asks if capitalism is the economic model that should be proposed to developing, third-world countries. He admits the answer is complex and says it depends on what you mean by "capitalism." He writes:

> If by "capitalism" is meant an economic system which recognizes the fundamental and positive role of business, the market, private property, and the resulting responsibility for the means of production, as well as free human creativity in the economic sector, then the answer is certainly in the affirmative, even though it would perhaps be more appropriate to speak of a "business economy," "market economy," or simply "free economy" (42).

John Paul did not directly call this system *capitalism*, but the name is still appropriate. When people are free to sell services and goods in the marketplace and can retain profits for their good and the good of their company, then capital will naturally accumulate. However, the pope goes on to say:

> But if by "capitalism" is meant a system in which freedom in the economic sector is not circumscribed within a

strong juridical framework which places it at the service of human freedom in its totality, and which sees it as a particular aspect of that freedom, the core of which is ethical and religious, then the reply is certainly negative (42).

A THIRD WAY?

Although capitalism is subject to abuse when it operates without legal limits, John Paul II stressed that "the Church's social doctrine is not a 'third way' between liberal capitalism and Marxist collectivism" (*Sollicitudo Rei Socialis* 41). The Church's social doctrine isn't economics or even a system of "Catholic economics." The search for this supposed third-way alternative to capitalism and Communism, which some Catholics see as necessary, actually involves a logical mistake that can be best understood through a theological analogy.

It is heretical to say either that Jesus is God but not man (as the Docetists did) or that he is man but not God (as the Arians did). But that doesn't mean there is a "third way" that splits the difference, understanding Christ to be half God and half man. The only acceptable formula is to believe that Jesus is fully God and fully man and that there is no contradiction in one person possessing two distinct natures, one fully human and the other fully divine.

Likewise, Pope Pius XI warned of social heresies like individualism, which denies that property ever has a public purpose, and collectivism (i.e., Communism), which denies it ever has a private purpose. But the Church does not advocate a "third way" in which property is considered half private and half public, or split in some other proportion between the two. Instead, Christian tradition had always taught that property has *both* a fully private and fully public character.

Property is meant to *serve its public character by means of private ownership.* This places enormous moral obligations on individuals and property owners to put their wealth at the service of the common good, an application of which we will see in our discussion of what constitutes a "just wage."

IT'S IMPORTANT TO REMEMBER . . .

- The problem of socialism spurred the Church to develop its modern social doctrine, addressing questions of political and economic justice.

- The science of economics is a matter for economists, not popes. Catholic social doctrine offers moral principles but not a comprehensive "Catholic economics" that the faithful must follow.

- Still less does the Church mandate a "middle way" that splits the difference between capitalism and socialism.

15

THE CHURCH ON JUST WAGES

In 1 Timothy 5:18, St. Paul defends paying priests a salary for their work by citing the words of Jesus: "The laborer deserves his wages" (Luke 10:7). Employers must pay workers what they were promised, and unjustly holding back these wages is the sin of wage theft. St. James has a frightful message for these sinners: "Behold, the wages of the laborers who mowed your fields, which you kept back by fraud, cry out; and the cries of the harvesters have reached the ears of the Lord of hosts" (5:4).

But there is more to the Church's teaching on what constitutes a just wage than merely keeping a promise to pay someone (CCC 2434). In *Rerum Novarum,* Leo XIII reminds employers that the most important thing they must give an employee is not a wage, per se, but *respect* as a human being.

WRONG PRINCIPLES FOR RIGHT WAGES

Leo says that "to misuse men as though they were things in the pursuit of gain, or to value them solely for their physical powers—that is truly shameful and inhuman." Workers are not mere instruments that produce labor for a company. Employers owe them fair conditions along with fair wages, which includes conditions that support the worker's spiritual good:

The employer is bound to see that the worker has time for his religious duties; that he be not exposed to corrupting influences and dangerous occasions; and that he be not led away to neglect his home and family, or to squander his earnings. Furthermore, the employer must never tax his work people beyond their strength, or employ them in work unsuited to their sex and age. (*Rerum Novarum* 20)

In the forty years that elapsed between *Rerum Novarum* and *Quadragesimo Anno,* Pius XI noted how the state passed numerous laws, unknown in Leo's time, that mandated these fair conditions. These laws "undertake the protection of life, health, strength, family, homes, workshops, wages, and labor hazards, *in fine*, everything which pertains to the condition of wage workers, with special concern for women and children" (*Quadragesimo Anno* 28).

Leo says the employers' "great and principal duty is to give everyone what is just" which includes right conditions along with right wages (*Rerum Novarum* 20). Justice means giving people what they deserve and though it's obvious that laborers deserve their wages, it's less clear what makes any particular wage just or unjust.

For example, Leo rejects the idea that the only just wage is the one a worker agrees to receive. This may be the case for certain personal kinds of labor (like agreeing to fix a friend's fence) that are be done for little or no money at all. But because labor is primarily ordered toward man's self-preservation, "there underlies a dictate of natural justice more imperious and ancient than any bargain between man and man, namely, that wages ought not to be insufficient to support a frugal and well behaved wage-earner" (45). Because God gave human beings labor as a way to provide for their own existence, it follows that there must be a way for people to support themselves through honest work. The fruit of labor is meant to benefit the worker in this way, but that fruit does not solely belong to the worker.

On the other hand, Pius XI dismisses the Marxist "labor theory of value" that says a worker is simply entitled to all the surplus value of his work. Pius calls it a "fictitious moral principle" that claims "all products and profits, save only enough to repair and renew capital, belong by very right to the workers" (*Quadragesimo Anno* 55). According to this fictitious principle, if a worker makes a pair of shoes that are sold for $50, he is entitled to that sum minus expenses and overheads. Pius says approaches like these are "shallow" because those who peddle them "think this most difficult matter [about wages] is easily solved by the application of a single rule or measure—and one quite false" (67).

We'll talk more about the labor of theory of value in the next chapter, but for now you can see this theory is flawed because it denies the employer the right to be compensated for the risks he takes in creating and operating the shoe company. Pius speaks of these entrepreneurs as representing "property" interests because they own property like factories, whereas workers represent "labor" interests. Pius says that "it is wholly false to ascribe to property alone or to labor alone whatever has been obtained through the combined effort of both, and it is wholly unjust for either, denying the efficacy of the other, to arrogate to itself whatever has been produced" (53).

Instead, this value must be divided between the parties and, although the Church does not give an exact formula for how to do this, it does give principles that set upper and lower limits for wages.

FAIR PRINCIPLES FOR FAIR WAGES

Concerning the upper limit for wages, Pius says that "it would be unjust to demand excessive wages which a business cannot stand without ruin and consequent calamity to the workers." If a company reduces wages because of its own mismanagement, he adds, they are morally responsible for the harm that befalls its workers. But, if an external pressure forces companies to, for example, "sell its product at less than a just price," then companies are not morally responsible for providing less-fair wages. Instead, it is the parties who exerted these unfair external pressures that are to blame. Moreover, there must be an upper limit to wages in order to preserve a kind of equilibrium in the workforce that provides "suitable means of livelihood . . . to the greatest possible number." Pius explains how

> the opportunity to work [ought] be provided to those who are able and willing to work. This opportunity depends largely on the wage and salary rate, which can help as long as it is kept within proper limits, but which on the other hand can be an obstacle if it exceeds these limits. For everyone knows that an excessive lowering of wages, or their increase beyond due measure, causes unemployment (*Quadragesimo Anno* 74).

When wages are too low, people don't have incentive to work and thus they remain unemployed. But when wages are too high, employers may reduce their operating costs by hiring fewer workers.

Even though labor is not merely a commodity, the price for a person's labor does behave like the prices for other goods. When a certain kind of labor skill is relatively rare (like dishwasher repair and maintenance) the price to buy this labor is higher than the price for more-common labor skills (like dishwashing). Catholic social doctrine strikes a balance between paying someone for the objective value of his labor (which is always a function of the overall supply of labor) and insuring that his basic human needs are met. The *Catechism* says,

> In determining fair pay both the needs and the contributions of each person must be taken into account. Remuneration for work should guarantee man the opportunity to provide a dignified livelihood for himself and his family on the material, social, cultural, and spiritual level, taking into account the role and the productivity of each, the state of the business, and the common good (CCC 2434).

Pope Leo said that "the worker must be paid a wage sufficient to support him and his family." But in a modern economy, it's not possible for every single occupation to pay a "family wage" that can support a spouse and children. The federal minimum wage, for example, is about half or a third of a family wage that can support dependents in most places.

For popes like Leo XIII and Pius XI, the answer to this dilemma is not found in a simple government policy like a law mandating a family wage for all jobs, which would raise unemployment to obscene levels. Leo proposes that, following the principle of subsidiarity, workers should seek just wages through organized bodies like labor unions, with state intervention being a last resort to ensure they are treated justly (*Rerum Novarum* 45). The pope sees unions operating under Christian principles as the best replacement for defunct guilds (which in the Middle Ages kept wages higher by restricting competition) and adds:

CAN A CATHOLIC BE A SOCIALIST?

The state should watch over these societies of citizens banded together in accordance with their rights, but it should not thrust itself into their peculiar concerns and their organization, for things move and live by the spirit inspiring them, and may be killed by the rough grasp of a hand from without (55).

Pius warns that these incursions into the market can be bad for the state as well as workers. If the state took over every labor issue that used to belong to guilds and unions, it would be "overwhelmed and crushed by almost infinite tasks and duties" (*Quadragesimo Anno* 78). Such incursions would also fail to respect "the role and the productivity of each [worker], the state of the business, and the common good," so a more complex solution is required to make sure that a worker's needs are met without disrupting the common good of society.

IT'S IMPORTANT TO REMEMBER . . .

- Catholic teaching on fair wages is based on principles of justice, not on the theory that a laborer is entitled to all the fruits of his labor.

- The Church recognizes that just wages take into account the legitimate interests of labor and ownership, which both play an indispensable role in the creation of wealth.

- Leo XIII and Pius XI believed that organized bodies of workers, such as labor unions, negotiating with ownership, is a better way to achieve just wages than state intervention.

16
CAPITALISM AND HUMAN LABOR

Some critics of capitalism say it is unjust to expect people to work for any wage, be it high or low. One critic claims, "The ruthless emphasis on profits over people [leads to] the proliferation of wage slavery—in which people have no choice but to sell their labor."[180] The "wage slavery" argument asserts that there is no morally relevant difference between forcing a person to work under the threat of punishment (i.e., traditional slavery) and forcing a person to work under the threat of withholding the wages he needs to survive.

The anarchist Emma Goldman once compared working for a wage to working for a slave owner, saying, "The only difference is that you are hired slaves instead of block [auction-bought] slaves."[181] Noam Chomsky agrees, saying, "It's not an odd view, that there isn't much difference between selling yourself and renting yourself."[182] These kinds of arguments are common among socialists, especially anarchist socialists who believe human beings should not have to submit to any authority. But they aren't persuasive because, as Leo XIII said, they don't "see the world as it really is."

THE MYTH OF "WAGE SLAVERY"

Slave owners in the antebellum South made the same basic argument as Chomsky, saying that if blacks could be "forced" to work in Northern factories for wages then there was nothing wrong with forcing them to work on Southern plantations.[183] But obviously there is a difference between working for a master and working for an employer. Slaves can't quit and choose to work for another master, but wageworkers can. Not only does this respect human freedom, unlike slavery, but it also encourages employers to compete for their labor and helps raise wages over time.

"Wage slavery" is really just an obtuse way of saying that people have to work even if they don't want to, because the alternative is starvation. This objection also assumes that capitalists never have to worry about money because they own the means of production. But factories don't produce money; they produce goods, and if no one buys what the capitalist offers then he can't support himself either.

Comparatively few people want to undertake the risks and long hours that most business owners face. That's why most of us choose to work for someone else, someone who has taken on those entrepreneurial risks for us. Does the fact that we choose not to live off the land or run our own business (or are unable to) in order to survive really make us slaves? On the other hand, the economist Bryan Caplan says that if society can take all of your excess wealth and redistribute it, then you would essentially be a slave, since in exchange for their labor slaves are only given enough to survive.[184]

EXPLOITATIVE WORK?

Even if we aren't "wage slaves," many other critics say that jobs under capitalism still exploit workers, since work is by its nature onerous. Marx said that modern industries "destroy every remnant of charm in his work and turn it into a hated toil."[185] Socialist journalism professor Robert Jensen laments that "the jobs we do are not rewarding, not enjoyable, and fundamentally not worth doing. We do them to survive. Then on Friday we go out and get drunk to forget about that reality."[186]

Except, when we look at actual data, this isn't true.

In 1830, Americans in manufacturing jobs worked close to seventy hours a week.[187] But as companies increased their production output that number dropped to sixty hours in 1890 and then to forty-two hours in 1930.[188] And while the number of hours has remained at that level, the number of Americans who reported being completely or somewhat satisfied with their job has continued to rise, going from 79 percent in 1993 to 90 percent in 2018.[189]

What about developing countries? Some socialists claim we are only able to work less because capitalism exploits poor workers abroad. Jensen says we should "put this in a global context. Half the world's population lives on less than $2 a day. That's more than three billion people."[190] But this is like blaming a firefighter because he was only able to keep half the house from burning down. If he hadn't shown up, the entire home would be in ashes, and the same is true when it comes to capitalism and global poverty.

In 1820, 94 percent of people lived on the equivalent of less than $2 a day, and for all previous human history that figure was probably closer to 99 percent.[191] Today, it is not half of people that live in such extreme poverty (as Jensen claims), but 10 percent.[192] That's still hundreds of millions of people who are suffering, but capitalism shouldn't be blamed for this, but rather be given credit for doing in 200 years what the human race couldn't achieve in the previous 20,000.

Indeed, areas of extreme poverty around the world need *more* capitalism, not less.

FREE MARKETS AND PROSPEROUS PEOPLE

In 1990, 60 percent of people in East Asia lived in extreme poverty, higher even than sub-Sahara Africa. By 2015, less than 3 percent of East Asia experienced extreme poverty while southern African poverty was still stuck at around 40 percent.[193] Capitalism explains much of this difference. East Asian "tiger economies" like Taiwan, Singapore, and South Korea (along with China, a latecomer to some free market activity) respect private property rights and have allowed businesses to grow and flourish. But in many sub-Saharan African countries, socialism, corruption, and government incompetence have combined to repress property rights and stifle the generation of wealth.

As Greg Mills describes in his book *Why Africa Is Poor,* the nation of Zambia suffered for three decades under the policies of the socialist UNIP party and its president Kenneth Kaunda. Mills shows how

> Kaunda's socialism has created a civil service geared to protectionism and regulation at all costs, and a private sector attuned to working within a system that rewards insiders and discourages independent entrepreneurship. (We should not underestimate the fact that this system, a feature of most African countries, works just fine for the elite.)[194]

Critics often point to manufacturing sweatshops and other harsh working conditions in Asian countries as evidence that capitalism is evil. And in many cases there certainly is room for making those conditions more just and humane. But we must also bear in mind that for many of these workers the alternatives are even worse. The economist Paul Kruger points out that when sweatshops in Bangladesh stopped hiring children, the "displaced child workers ended up in even worse jobs, or on the streets—and that a significant number were forced into prostitution."[195] What the Austrian economist Ludwig von Mises said of nineteenth-century factory workers is still true for many workers around the world today:

> It is a distortion of facts to say that the factories carried off the housewives from the nurseries and the kitchens and the children from their play. These women had nothing to cook with and to feed their children. These children were destitute and starving. Their only refuge was the factory. It saved them, in the strict sense of the term, from death by starvation.[196]

Many people today labor under unjust or undignified conditions. The solution to their suffering, however, is to *improve* those conditions, not do away with the economic system that offers the best chance to provide those improvements. To that end, we should remember the old saying, "Do not make the perfect the enemy of the good."

NO EASY SOLUTIONS

When Marxist sociologist Erik Olin Wright quipped that "the hallmark of capitalism is poverty in the midst of plenty," he did have a point. We should be upset when some people don't have enough to eat while others eat so much that it becomes a health problem. The title of Ronald Sider's 1978 book on poverty—*Rich Christians in an Age of Hunger*—is a gut punch for people of faith. But we must remember that capitalism did not create poverty among the wealthy: it created wealthy people among the poor.

Poverty was the normal existence for 99 percent of all human beings before the Industrial Revolution, and since that time poverty levels around the globe have fallen. The

reason poverty persists is not primarily an economic problem; it's a moral problem. This is why Popes Leo XIII and
Pius XI emphasized the so-called "social question," which
is the problem of poverty.

This wasn't a new question because poverty was new—it
was a new question because with modern economic growth
not all men were poor. Since there were now more people who
were not poor and more people who were rich, the "problem" was how the new, relatively wealthy were supposed to
use their wealth (to provide relief to the poor) and how the
poor were to bear their lot (that is, not agitate for socialism).
Whence, in relation to the newly wealthy, Pope Pius XI said:

> A person's superfluous income, that is, income which he
> does not need to sustain life fittingly and with dignity,
> is not left wholly to his own free determination. Rather
> the sacred scriptures and the Fathers of the Church con-
> stantly declare in the most explicit language that the rich
> are bound by a very grave precept to practice almsgiving,
> beneficence, and munificence (*Quadragesimo Anno* 50).

People have a moral obligation to use their excess wealth
to help those who cannot even afford the basic necessities of
life. But the Church also teaches that the state should not legally enforce all of our moral obligations. Imagine if it was a
crime to break any promise or tell any lie. The evils created
by a state that meddled in every aspect of our lives would be
worse than the evils it tried to eliminate. St. Thomas Aquinas said on this matter:

> The purpose of human law is to lead men to virtue, not
> suddenly, but gradually. Wherefore it does not lay upon the
> multitude of imperfect men the burdens of those who are

already virtuous, viz. that they should abstain from all evil. Otherwise these imperfect ones, being unable to bear such precepts, would break out into yet greater evils.[197]

Our study of history shows that the same is true when the state uses socialist policies to force people to carry out their duty to help the poor. Socialists have never succeeded in creating the classless, poverty-free worker's paradise they perpetually promise to the impoverished who put their hope in them. Instead, their collectivist solutions simply increase poverty for everyone—except for leaders who end up having more than they need.

As we will see in our examination of the modern "return of socialism," what Winston Churchill said sixty years ago is still true today: "The inherent vice of capitalism is the unequal sharing of blessings. The inherent virtue of socialism is the equal sharing of miseries."[198]

IT'S IMPORTANT TO REMEMBER . . .

- The idea that working for a wage is "slavery" is a myth. In a fallen world we all must work even if we don't want to—even the owners of the means of production.

- Far from worsening the conditions of "wage slaves," modern capitalism has made labor much less burdensome and much more remunerative.

- In places where people still labor in comparative poverty, evidence suggests that economic freedom rather than collectivist control offers the best chance for the development necessary to lift them out of poverty.

PART FIVE

SOCIALISM RECONSTRUCTED

17
THE NORDIC MYTH

There was once a group of mice that wanted a solution to the cat who constantly hunted them. One mouse proposed that a bell be tied around the cat's neck to provide them with a warning whenever it was near. The other mice applauded his plan until an older mouse spoke up and said, "Yes, but who will bell the cat?"

One collection of fables describes the lesson to be learned: *it is easy to propose impossible remedies.* The same lesson applies to socialism.

Like belling the cat, the rewards and goal are easy to explain. They want to eliminate poverty by planning the economy and redistributing wealth. But the mechanism to achieve the goal isn't spelled out, because it can't be done. Central planners can never efficiently meet diverse consumer needs, which is something all the failed socialist states we've examined in this book prove beyond doubt.

"But they didn't practice true socialism!" the critic responds.

Well, if they weren't practitioners of "true socialism," then who is?

Socialists know that they can't be taken seriously if they can't provide even one example of their theory working in real life. That's why when critics ask them about China, North Korea, and the Soviet Union, they usually reply in kind by asking, "What about Denmark, Norway, and Sweden? They practice *democratic socialism* and they have the highest living standards in the world!"

(NON-) SOCIALIST SCANDINAVIA

In her Catholic defense of democratic socialism, Brianne Jacobs says young people are not afraid of socialism because, unlike their parents, they don't associate socialism with threats to freedom like the Soviet Union. Instead, "We tend to associate socialism with democracies: Sweden, Norway, Denmark, Finland—countries that have low economic inequality and a high quality of life, achieved through universal social programs and financed through high tax rates."[199]

But remember that social welfare, or government spending on the poor, is not the same as socialism, or government planning of the economy. Nordic countries have generous social welfare programs, but they are nowhere near socialism because they have a robust system of private property protections.

According to the Heritage Foundation's economic freedom index, Hong Kong and Singapore are the most capitalist economies on earth while North Korea and Venezuela are the most socialist. In between these two extremes, you have countries with mixed models like France, which ranks 70 out of 180 when it comes to economic freedom. This is probably due to that country's "indicative planning" that relies on government *persuasion* to plan the economy through things like grants and tax breaks instead of government *coercion* through socialist policies like price controls and production quotas.[200]

So where do the Nordic countries fall on the economic freedom index?

Denmark, Sweden, Finland, and Norway rank fourteen, nineteen, twenty, and twenty-six respectively.[201] Compared with the rest of the world, they have relatively free markets and are much more like the United States (which ranks twelfth) than socialist Venezuela (which ranks at 177). When Denmark was held up as an example of socialism in the 2015 presidential primary debates, the prime minister of Denmark said in response:

> I know that some people in the U.S. associate the Nordic model with some sort of socialism. Therefore I would like to make one thing clear. Denmark is far from a so-cialist planned economy. Denmark is a market economy. The Nordic model is an expanded welfare state which provides a high level of security for its citizens, but it is also a successful market economy with much freedom to pursue your dreams and live your life as you wish.[202]

ECONOMIC TRADEOFFS

It's understandable why so many people are attracted to Nordic economic models. They claim to offer free college, free health care, generous minimum wages, along with vacation plans and retirement benefits for workers. These countries also have relatively low poverty rates and come in at the top of lists that rank countries by the quality of life they provide for their citizens. But economic models always involve trading one kind of good for another kind of good, and the Nordic model is no exception.

Unlike with socialism, Catholics can reasonably disagree over whether the Nordic model should be replicated in oth-er countries, but that debate should highlight some of the tradeoffs inherent in these models as well as misconceptions people have about them, such as:

- Nordic countries do not have minimum wage laws. Their higher wages are usually the result of collective bargaining agreements between unions and employers, which, you'll recall, was Pope Leo XIII's preferred alternative to government regulation.[203]

- Nordic countries have very high tax rates and their citizens have lower average incomes than citizens in countries like Japan or the United States.[204]

- Nordic countries have some of the longest wait times to see medical providers, which may explain why the number of private health insurance plans doubled in Sweden between 2006 and 2011.[205]

- Although Nordic schools, including colleges, do not charge tuition, they often charge high fees, and students still accumulate debt because of the region's high cost of living.[206] Education options are also limited, which can be seen in the non-existence of private schools in Finland and the illegality of homeschooling in Sweden.[207]

- Welfare states like those in Scandinavia can experience slower economic growth when immigration rates increase.[208] Consequently, these countries have to make a choice between reducing social services or reducing the number of immigrants they are willing to accept into the country.

In some cases, these tradeoffs would make these models impermissible from a Catholic perspective. These include policies that forbid parents from providing their children with religious education by outlawing home and parochial schools in favor of government education. But in other cases they can represent a legitimate model Catholics may support, provided that these models are not employed as a path to socialism.

THE SCALING PROBLEM

Economic models cannot be applied universally and, at certain scales, they stop working. Centralizing food storage and allocating it based on individual need works great for a single-family home or even a small religious community. But such a model would be impractical for entire neighborhoods and, as history grimly reminds us, can be fatal for entire countries. The same is true for some national economic policies, which can work in smaller, more homogenous countries whose citizens share similar values but may become unwieldy in larger, more diverse ones.

Monaco and Luxembourg have even higher standards of living than the Nordic countries, but they only have populations of 40,000 and 600,000 people respectively. After the 2008 financial crisis, Barack Obama was asked about copying Sweden's plan to nationalize banks in order to protect them from insolvency due to bad investments. In response, President Obama said, "Sweden looks like a good model. Here's the problem: Sweden had like five banks. We've got thousands of banks. You know, the scale of the U.S. economy and the capital markets are so vast . . . it wouldn't make sense."[209]

Among countries that have more than 100 million citizens, Japan and the United States rank first and second when it comes to providing people with a high quality of life.[210] Of course, when a country has both a large geographic area and a high population, there can be dramatic differences in the quality of life people enjoy in the various cities in that country. But the cities across the globe with the highest quality of life tend to be found in free democracies, whereas the worst cities in the world, such as Lagos, Nigeria and Caracas, Venezuela, tend to be found in countries that restrict both personal and economic freedoms.[211] As we turn in the next chapter to the reality of what happens when countries fully embrace socialist policies, you'll see why Venezuela earns this failing grade.

IT'S IMPORTANT TO REMEMBER . . .

- Claims that "democratic socialism" in Scandinavian countries has successfully combined state economic control with prosperity and social stability tend to ignore basic facts about how their economies actually work.

- Economic and political models that are reasonably successful on small scales—a family, a town, even a small nation—often do not translate to larger scales.

- These "Nordic models" also come with tradeoffs, some of which would be intolerable from a Catholic perspective.

18
THE VENEZUELAN
REALITY

In the 1970s, Venezuela was one of the richest, most stable countries in Latin America, due in large part to its vast oil reserves. The government's revenue quadrupled during the 1973 oil crisis and politicians made plans like *La Gran Venezuela* that would nationalize the oil industry and allow the country to splurge on public entitlement programs. According to journalist Michael McCaughan, "Venezuelan workers enjoyed the highest wages in Latin America and subsidies in food, health, education, and transport sectors."[212]

But when oil prices began to decline in the 1980s, so did the Venezuelan economy.

By the late 1990s, worker income was half of what it had been in the 1970s, and riots in the city's capital of Caracas left hundreds dead.[213] In 1998, populist presidential candidate Hugo Chavez promised to use Venezuela's oil reserves for the benefit of the poor and campaigned on the slogan, "Motherland, Socialism, or Death."[214] Chavez won the election with 56 percent of the vote, most of it coming from the country's poor and middle-class citizens. He appointed his own advisers to lead the country's oil industry, which subsequently became a piggy bank from which Chavez spent lavishly on social programs. In a speech he gave to the World Fund he declared:

We must transcend capitalism. But we cannot resort to state capitalism, which would be the same perversion of the Soviet Union. We must reclaim socialism as a thesis, a project, and a path, but a new type of socialism, a humanist one, which puts humans and not machines or the state ahead of everything.[215]

¡VIVA CHAVEZ!

In the early 2000s, Chavez launched a series of welfare programs called "missions" that provided subsidized food and free medical care to impoverished citizens. One 2006 report showed that the programs helped Chavez win reelection, but problems were already starting to emerge with the demand they created. The reporter observed "long lines form outside the supermarkets known as *Mercals,*" with a "mother of three shout[ing] at security guards keeping her waiting for an hour." However, the mother admitted she would still vote for Chavez because, "He's giving us all these benefits and needs our support . . . so he can keep giving more benefits."[216]

In order to keep the welfare system functioning, Chavez initiated price controls on staples like rice, milk, and meat. He ordered companies that produced these goods both to sell them at low prices and increase their production in order to meet consumer demand. When the companies complained that they would go out of business by being forced to sell goods at such low prices, Chavez sent his troops in to make sure they would comply. When that didn't work, he had the government take over the businesses through a process called *expropriation*.

According to a 2019 feature in the *Washington Post*, "In two decades, the government seized nearly five million acres of productive farmland that has now been largely abandoned. In 1999, there were 490,000 private companies in Venezuela. By last June—the most recent count available—that number had fallen to 280,000."[217] Venezuela also drove out foreign oil companies and nationalized domestic steel, glass, and food production. A 2010 article in *The Economist* described how a typical "expropriation" occurs with the example of Owens Illinois, an American-owned bottle manufacturer:

> In his usual style, Mr. Chavez offhandedly slipped the announcement into the middle of a speech lasting several hours, which all radio and television stations were required to carry . . . Owens Illinois was given no advance warning of the measure, and new management entered the factory just a few days after it was announced.[218]

The article goes to describe how Chavez was committed to "the elimination of capitalism" and that he "believes individuals should be entitled to their personal belongings, but not control of the means of production." But although in theory "the people" owned the means of production, it was the state that controlled the factories that produced the goods. And without any profit motivation, their production rates steadily declined until Venezuela went from being a country that produced most of its own food to one that imported most of it.[219]

In spite of these moves, Venezuela was still surviving economically because of oil prices that went (when adjusted for inflation) from $19 a barrel when Chavez was first elected to nearly $100 a barrel when he died in 2013. In the wake of his death, journalists, academics, and celebrities lionized Chavez and praised Venezuela as evidence that socialism can work if it's "done right."

A BETTER WORLD

Remember that, at this point, hardly anyone doubted that Venezuela represented "true socialism." The economy was centrally planned, the government abolished large sectors of private industry, such as factories and farms, and the wealth produced from these resources was redistributed among the people, just as with every other socialist country in history.

Noam Chomsky visited the country in 2009 and said, "What's so exciting about at last visiting Venezuela is that I can see how a better world is being created."[220] David Sirota of Salon.com admitted "Chavez was no saint" due to his authoritarian policies but he still called the Venezuelan economy "a miracle" that can teach us how to alleviate poverty.[221] *Jacobin* magazine likewise praised Venezuela's reduction in poverty and said, "Today we mourn the death of Chavez, tomorrow we return to the grind for socialism."[222]

When conditions deteriorated after Chavez's death and lines to buy items like toilet paper started to emerge, economist Mark Weisbrot called those who predicted disaster "haters" who had "cried wolf." He asked, "How can a government with more than $90bn in oil revenue end up with a balance-of-payments crisis?" His answer: "It can't, and won't."[223]

Weisbrot had also served as an adviser to Oliver Stone's 2009 film *South of the Border,* which portrayed Latin American socialism as an economic boon to the region and its socialist leaders as friendly rulers that people would love if they got to know them. In one scene, Chavez rides a bicycle in his grandmother's backyard but the bicycle collapses under his weight—a prophetic symbol of the Venezuelan economy.

When Chavez died, filmmaker Michael Moore wrote on social media, "Hugo Chavez declared the oil belonged to the people. He used the oil money to eliminate 75 percent of extreme poverty, provide free health care and education for all."[224] Stone simply said that Chavez "will live forever in history."[225]

CONSEQUENCES AND EXCUSES

From 2014 to 2016, oil prices dropped from $110 a barrel to less than $40, gutting Venezuela's economy. Without ample revenue from oil exports, the government had to cut back on its social programs and could no longer subsidize its thousands of nationalized industries.

The electric companies, which were supposed to provide "free electricity" for the people, were now experiencing weekly blackouts.[226] The national water company made similar promises of cheap utilities, but because it had no incentive to invest in its infrastructure, water pumps failed and people in the capital of Caracas could only access water for about an hour a day.[227] Food also became scarce because imports necessary to offset the loss of domestic food production were now too expensive.

In 2016, the government tried to offset the shortage by passing a law allowing it to force people to engage in agricultural work. Not only was this repressive and hypocritical according to socialism's alleged "pro-worker" ideals, it was also futile. As a director of the human rights organization Amnesty International said in response, "Trying to tackle Venezuela's severe food shortages by forcing people to work the fields is like trying to fix a broken leg with a band aid."[228]

Indeed, grocery store shelves remain empty. In 2017, the average Venezuelan lost 24 pounds, thanks to what the locals wryly dubbed the "Venezuelan diet."[229] The country has refused to release medical statistics since 2013, but outside researchers estimate infant mortality has increased by about 50 percent, to a level that hadn't been seen in nearly two decades.[230] Chavez's successor Nicholas Maduro tried to solve the problem by printing more money, but this led to hyper-inflation, making Venezuelan currency essentially worthless.

By 2019, the Venezuelan economy was half of what it had been under Chavez and inflation rates were at nearly ten million percent.[231] Maduro raised the country's minimum wage to 18,000 bolivars, which in previous years would have been equivalent to $3,000. However, because the bolivar wasn't worth the paper it was printed on, this monthly minimum wage was equivalent to six U.S. dollars; enough to buy three pounds of chicken.[232] With the currency now worthless, people resorted to bartering to get what they needed. Taxi rides were paid in cigarettes and you could get a haircut for five bananas and two eggs.[233]

Defenders of socialism have come up with a variety of excuses for the Venezuelan crisis that try to place the blame on anything but socialism. Most point to falling oil prices; but that doesn't explain how countries with similar dependencies on oil exports, like Kuwait and Saudi Arabia, managed to avoid economic catastrophe. Others blamed the collapse on "mismanagement," but that's just a variation on the claim that when socialism fails it's because it wasn't "true" (properly managed) socialism. Yet the reality is, that's what *always* happens in socialist economies. Instead of allowing prices to be set by natural consumer demand and realistic business supply, socialist governments like Venezuela set price controls and production quotas that can't be sustained. Socialism is mismanagement by definition.

Since 2014, four million Venezuelans have fled the country, resulting in the largest displacement of people in recent Latin-American history.[234] In an editorial with the headline, "Venezuela was my home, and socialism destroyed it. Slowly, it will destroy America, too," Venezuelan expatriate Daniel Di Martino calls the government's excuses for the country's woes "hollow." He writes, "Venezuela has the largest proven oil reserves in the world to use for electricity, and three times more fresh water resources per person than the United States. The real reason my family went without water and electricity was the socialist economy instituted by dictators Hugo Chavez and Nicolas Maduro."[235]

IT'S IMPORTANT TO REMEMBER . . .

- Venezuela is an object lesson in how even a relatively wealthy economy blessed with natural resources can be decimated by state collectivization—even when it is done in the name of humanitarianism.

- The hyperinflation, degradation of industry and agriculture, and political repression that socialism brought to Venezuela are features, not bugs, of that economic system.

19
DEBUNKING CATHOLIC SOCIALISM

In Dostoevsky's 1880 novel *The Brothers Karamazov,* a police-man says he is not afraid of atheists, revolutionaries, and other socialists. But he does fear "a few peculiar men among them who believe in God and are Christians, but at the same time are socialists. These are the people we are most afraid of. They are dreadful people! The socialist who is a Christian is more to be dreaded than a socialist who is an atheist."[236]

No matter how hard atheistic regimes try to create heaven on earth, they can't extinguish the natural desire to worship the divine. So when socialists try to stamp out religion, even nominally faithful people recoil in horror. A far more insidi-ous problem arises when socialists co-opt religious language to make it seem like their crusade is in complete harmony with—or even required by—Christian values.

Dean Dettloff's "The Catholic Case for Communism," published in the official Jesuit magazine *America*, is prob-ably the most conspicuous recent example. Another was the *Tradinista Manifesto* published in 2016 by a group of young Catholics committed to "the destruction of capitalism, and its replacement by a truly social political economy."[237]

The manifesto's name is a combination of traditionalist Catholicism that seeks the return of the Catholic state with the principles of the *Sandinistas*, a socialist political party in Nicaragua that came to prominence in the 1980s, were opposed by the U.S.-backed *Contras,* and dominates politics in that country today. Strangely absent in the manifesto, though, is any denunciation of the Sandinistas' mob violence, their practice of making political enemies "disappear," and the intimidation tactics they still use in opposition to the local Catholic Church's pro-democracy stance today.[238]

Far from being an obscure online publication, the document made the rounds on the internet and even got attention from the *New York Times* and the Catholic publication *First Things*, whose editor said, "When it comes to the Tradinistas, I think I'm not a contra."[239] But a closer examination of their defense of Catholic socialism reveals that it is certainly socialist but it isn't Catholic—or even plausible.

DOWN WITH CAPITALISM!

In the section of the manifesto on abolishing capitalism, we find this claim: "The foundational relation of capitalist society is between those who are compelled to sell their labor-power on pain of destitution and those who, by their ownership of capital, are enabled to exploit the former."

In fact, the foundational relation in capitalist societies is between *producers* and *consumers*, not owners and workers. There are, of course, villainous owners and toiling workers, but it is not true that they make up two classes within society that are at necessary war with each other. Instead, society consists of a network of people, each of whom produces goods and services and also consumes goods and services.

Consider a butcher who hires a plumber to fix his sink, for which he pays him $100. That evening, the plumber returns to buy $100 worth of meat to feed his family. Which one is "compelled to sell their labor-power on pain of destitution" and which is the evil capitalist who "exploits" a helpless worker? It looks like each of these men belongs to both groups, which means they actually belong to neither. The plumber and the butcher each owns means of production, but these means do not make them self-sufficient. They must offer something that is valuable to another person in order to obtain wages that they can spend on their livelihood.

Modern socialists who are obsessed with reviving Marx's arguments about exploitation of labor also neglect a dramatic change in the workforce since the publication of *The Communist Manifesto.* In 1910, 46 percent of the U.S. economy was devoted to producing goods through mining, farming, manufacturing, and construction. That percentage was probably higher in Marx's time, but even by the early twentieth century only 3 percent of workers were devoted to fields like information services, business services, health care, and social assistance. Today these "other services," as the Department of Labor calls them, make up the largest group of workers in the United States. Instead of working on farms or in factories, nearly one-third of all workers provide these services, in contrast to the 9 percent of workers involved in manufacturing.[240]

That's one reason why the manifesto's goal of doing away with "the capitalist class—which serves its own ends, detrimental to the common good of society" is wrongheaded. Economic development has led, not to two distinct, warring classes, but to a genuine interdependence among all human beings, of the sort that Pope Leo XIII discussed in *Rerum Novarum.*

NOTHING MORE THAN A SLAVE?

The *Tradinista Manifesto* also contains a fatal omission. It says workers are economically exploited because they "must sell their labor-power on the market in order to survive. While citizens should be free to engage in market exchange, the polity should ensure that no basic needs—food, clothing, shelter, health care, etc.—go unmet, guaranteeing a livelihood independent of the market."

One of the manifesto's authors, Jose Mena, says in another article that "Pope St. John XXIII teaches that the rights of man include the basic necessities of life—medical care, food and shelter, rest—independent of anyone's ability to secure these through labor. Is this not socialism?"[241] It isn't, because here is what Pope John XXIII *actually* said:

> Man has the right to live. He has the right to bodily integrity and to the means necessary for the proper development of life, particularly food, clothing, shelter, medical care, rest, and, finally, the necessary social services. In consequence, he has the right to be looked after in the event of ill health; disability stemming from his work; widowhood; old age; enforced unemployment; or whenever *through no fault of his own* [emphasis added] he is deprived of the means of livelihood (*Pacem in Terris* 11).

No one should be deprived of his basic needs simply because he can't work. Charity, and to some extent government programs, should provide these resources to those who cannot work—such as the sick or the disabled. But that's a far cry from saying that *all people* should have their basic needs met independent of having to work for others. After all, basic needs like food, clothing, and medicine have to be produced by *someone,* and so the question in the socialist system becomes, "Who gets tasked with that job?"

In his critique of the *Tradinista Manifesto*, Matthew Shadle engages one of its authors, C.W. Strand, who attempts to resolve this problem. Strand says that workers could be compelled by the state to create these goods by giving them "a diminution in their guaranteed, state-provided basic goods and services." In other words, those who don't work, or don't work enough, or don't perform the designated kind of work, will be cut off by the state from their share of communal goods. Which, when you think about it for more than three seconds, is just an oblique way of describing a totalitarian regime.

Instead of "sell[ing] their labor-power on the market in order to survive," then, the Tradinistas want a society where people must hand over their labor-power to the *state* in order to survive. Strand sees how this seems like state-run capitalism, but responds by claiming that, at least under socialism, the state compels people to work for the benefit of the common good, whereas under capitalism there is a "structural compulsion to work" that only benefits private interests. But Shadle notes the flaw in this argument:

> The "structural compulsion to work" is exactly the same under capitalism and socialism: people must work to produce a livelihood, one way or another. Tradinista socialism then adds the *further* compulsion of having to work for the state at risk of losing one's livelihood. So the problem with capitalism, for the Tradinistas, is not that people are *compelled* to work, but rather that they are compelled to work for *capitalists*.[242]

Moreover, unlike in most capitalist systems—where a person is free to work for another employer who offers better terms—under Catholic socialism you can either take the government's terms or enjoy the "diminution" of your rations. In the face of proposals like these, one is reminded of Ronald Reagan's eloquent criticism of socialism and its promises of free food, medicine, and all other necessities for just a little "communal work":

> Socialists ignore the side of man that is the spirit. They can provide you shelter, fill your belly with bacon and beans, treat you when you're ill, all the things guaranteed to a prisoner or a slave. They don't understand that we also dream."[243]

PUT NOT YOUR TRUST IN PRINCES

Poverty and unjust working conditions are real problems, and sometimes their root lies in an unjust and dysfunctional economic system—socialism being the example *par excellence*. But usually, societal injustices are the result of deeper moral evils like greed, envy, indifference, and selfishness. Simply reordering society so people aren't poor can't eliminate these vices (and doesn't solve poverty, either). That's the error of liberation theology which, as we've seen, unsuccessfully tries to wed Marxism and Christianity. The Congregation for the Doctrine of the Faith accordingly rebuked its central premise: that evil can be localized "principally or uniquely in bad social, political, or economic 'structures' as though all other evils came from them so that the creation of the 'new man' would depend on the establishment of different economic and socio-political structures."[244]

We believe that many people (including self-styled "Catholic socialists") support socialism because they believe that whereas private citizens are mostly self-interested, governments are altruistic. "Government" becomes almost a magical entity whose vast resources could solve all our problems if it was just put to work in the right way.

But governments are really just groups of individuals who have been given weighty responsibilities. Those individuals are not immune to the effects of vice; in fact, the temptations that government officials face make them *more* susceptible to sin and the magnitude of the problems they face make them *more* prone to error. The Psalmist presciently warned us, "Put not your trust in princes, in a son of man, in whom there is no help. When his breath departs he returns to his earth; on that very day his plans perish" (146:3–4).

Christians should strive toward making governments and societies more just, but it's fruitless to try and build a heaven on earth as long as human beings are the ones running this "heaven." Instead, the problem of poverty must be tackled at its root in the *poverty of virtue* that lies in people's hearts. In other words, we're not just dealing with honest mistakes about the economic and political order; we're looking at sin in the human heart. This is why the complete response to the "problem of the workers" (as *Rerum Novarum* is sometimes called) is both the right principles (including a rejection of socialism in all its forms) *and* a deeper conversion to the truth—the life of grace and the sacraments lived in the bosom of the Church.

Pope Leo opened *Rerum Novarum* saying that the socialists look to exploit the "poor man's envy of the rich" [4]. Envy, which springs from the feeling of sorrow or sadness at another person's good, seeks to diminish the good things of another. Thus, the socialists aren't merely jealous that some people have more than others—they seek to harness state power to take property away from those who have it and to destroy the institutions related to the protection of property. It is counted as a capital sin because of the other vices that arise from it, including hatred and violence.

What is needed in response, then, is not merely a superior system but repentance and grace. And we must begin with ourselves, examining how to live a godly life through the economic decisions we make every day.

IT'S IMPORTANT TO REMEMBER . . .

- Even today there are movements among progressive and traditional Catholics alike to rehabilitate socialism as an economic system in line with—or even required by—the gospel.

- Collectivist solutions to poverty and economic injustice substitute political fiat for the free and virtuous living-out of human interdependence.

- Government-controlled wealth redistribution exploits "the poor man's envy of the rich" to grow the power of the state at the expense of the Church, the family, and other institutions that we should trust and love more.

20
CATHOLICISM AND MORAL CAPITALISM

For some people, the aspiration to pursue "moral capitalism" sounds like the claim of being an "honest thief." Even those who know that capitalism is not intrinsically wrong may still imagine that walking the path of "moral capitalism" is like strolling along the edge of a cliff: step over the line too far in one direction or another and you might fall into exploitation, abuse, or greed.

But this isn't how the Church sees it, and it isn't how we should see it.

The reason that Church teaching has always stressed the importance of principles of right order is just this: so we can have confidence and peace that in applying ourselves with hard work and diligence we can joyfully participate in God's co-creation—a task we are urged to take up for the good of our families and our communities.

FOR WANT OF WANTS

Capitalism satisfies our desires to create and consume but, of itself, it cannot tutor or censor our wants. So, for instance, capitalism is a very effective way of satisfying the seemingly insatiable demand (want) for pornographic material, and this was true long before the internet age. Unlike greed, which

CAN A CATHOLIC BE A SOCIALIST?

finds a natural check of sorts in competitive markets, disordered, evil desires do not find a natural check.

This is why Michael Novak, Catholic philosopher and friend of John Paul II, wrote his greatest work, *The Spirit of Democratic Capitalism,* to talk about the "three-legged" stool that was needed for a healthy political economy, comprising: 1) free and democratic political order, 2) economy of free enterprise, and 3) virtuous citizens shaped by a sound moral order. Each of these, he believed, vitally depended upon a strong religious framework, and the absence of any of these elements would sabotage any economy.

For even if people are to vote, buy, and sell whatever they want, they can still enslave themselves to inhuman wants and desires. As St. Paul said, "If you yield yourselves to any one as obedient slaves, you are slaves of the one whom you obey, either of sin, which leads to death, or of obedience, which leads to righteousness?" (Rom. 6:16).

A good analogy to how we can practice moral capitalism is how we can morally relate to food. Modern economies have made food and drink nearly omnipresent. And since eating is pleasant, it is really easy to slide into a kind of "food-ism" analogous to consumerism. It can happen even without overeating or practicing the vice of gluttony in the traditional sense. We might think of ourselves as a "foodie" who becomes obsessed with our food, where it's made, what it will do to us, how much we will have, and when we will have it. Our sense of self becomes a little too wrapped up in what we eat and how we eat.

What goes into making this possible? The easy availability of an activity (or thing) that is pleasant, good for us, and intended by God for our joy. It's the same with our economic life. There was a time when we poked fun at businessmen clutching Blackberries with a whole keyboard at their palms.

Now we are all "that guy," and we have the capacity with a little device to engage in more economic transactions in ten minutes than merchants of Venice hoped for in a year's time.

Modern capitalism makes the temporary euphoria and pleasure associated with the activities of buying and selling a temptation to engage in too much, too often, to where it becomes an idol, wholly divorced from its purpose of serving virtue and the genuine human needs of ourselves and others. Buying and selling becomes our identity, or at least a place where we inadvertently deposit too much of our sense of security. *Whatever else happens today,* we may effectively think to ourselves, *at least I bought something.*

As sons and daughters of God, we are more than "producers," "consumers," "utility maximizers" or even "shoppers" (no matter many preferred customer membership cards are bloating our wallets). We are Christians, which means capitalism isn't a way of life, much less our identity. However optimistic we are about entrepreneurship, business, and free markets, economic values are not, and cannot be, the only values (*Centesimus Annus* 39).

So how do we practically break free from capitalism's consumerist temptations?

PUTTING THINGS DOWN

First, we have to notice and understand the temptation, which is the warping of a good thing. Just as food isn't the problem, but giving it too much importance *is*. Similarly, shopping, work, and market economies aren't the problem; giving it all too much importance makes it a problem.

Second, the task is to put things in order, which is also a way of putting ourselves and our souls in order. Putting things in order has been described as part of the virtue of justice, which is one reason why justice is not just *a* cardinal virtue but is *chief* among the cardinal virtues. The first task of social justice is to put ourselves into right order: in relation to ourselves, to our neighbor, and to God.

This is a simple exercise of the sort that children practice naturally—like putting blocks or rings of different sizes into place. The liturgical calendar is designed for us to do just this: We put food, or drink, or other pleasures, in their right place. We fast when a special occasion calls for it; and when things that are not God have creeped too high in our lives, we put them down and elevate prayer and penance above them. The wisdom of Ecclesiastes reminds us, "For everything there is a season, and a time for every matter under heaven . . . a time to mourn, and a time to dance; a time to cast away stones, and a time to gather stones together" (3:1,4).

We do this repeatedly year after year because we need it. We should trust this solution. It works—because it conforms to how we were made, and how we are able to be sanctified in the world.

The greatest prayer of the Church is the sacramental life: thus, the path to living morally within a market economy is to renew and exercise our commitment to grounding our identity in God who is the supreme and final good for us, and in the life of grace that the Church offers to us as a good mother. We can say with confidence: If prayer and the sacraments have the first place in our lives, we do not have to worry about falling off the consumerist cliff. Because we were made to be vessels of grace, and when we are filled with grace we are filled with virtue; and virtue, as the great saints have always shown, is a life of balance and stability.

WITH ALL OUR STRENGTH

To put this in relation to our lives in a market economy—whether we think about our role as buyers or sellers, workers or entrepreneurs, or members of the new creative class—at the very least we need to *fast from market activities* as often as sensible. This means spending more time reflecting on the ancient traditions.

Many traditional Christian cultures have discouraged shopping on Sunday. It's not that shopping is wrong—but that a fast helps put it in its place, and provides room for moving prayer and time spent outside the market higher in our lives. John Paul II said, "When Sunday loses its fundamental meaning and becomes merely part of a 'weekend,' it can happen that people stay locked within a horizon so limited that they can no longer see 'the heavens.' Hence, though ready to celebrate, they are really incapable of doing so" (*Dies Domine* 4).

Other ways of fasting from economic activity—or putting things in their place—include examining and rededicating ourselves to charitable giving. This also helps us fight the temptation to hoard money and goods once we accumulate a lot of them. Psychology researcher Paul Piff has shown that poor people are actually more charitable than the wealthy because they are better at identifying with the suffering of the poor and thus having compassion for them.[245] This leads them to make more sacrificial gifts than wealthy people who may only give away a small percentage of their wealth.

When you read this study you can't help but think of the widow who deposited two coins in the temple treasury while the rich deposited their abundant gifts. But Jesus tells us that the widow gave more than all of those rich men put together because "they all contributed out of their abundance, but she out of her poverty put in all the living that she had" (Luke 21:4).

In Deuteronomy 6:5, the Israelites were commanded, "Love the LORD your God with all your heart, and with all your soul, and with all your might [or strength]." The word for "might" is *meodekah* and probably referred to one's material possessions.[246] In both the ancient and modern world, a person's "strength" comes not from what he can bench press but from what he can purchase. We are commanded to love God with all our economic strength and to use that strength to love our neighbor as ourselves. When we don't, we incur the same condemnation Pope Pius XI gave to the stingy rich of his time that gave credence to the arguments of the socialists:

> It is certainly most lamentable, venerable brethren, that there have been, nay, that even now there are men who, although professing to be Catholics, are almost completely unmindful of that sublime law of justice and charity that binds us not only to render to everyone what is his but to succor brothers in need as Christ the Lord himself (*Quadragesimo Anno* 125).

But sacrifices cannot stop at just giving money to the needy (as important as that is). We can also sacrifice our felt need to buy things by making do with what we have for longer, repairing instead of replacing them. We can also sacrifice our time for the poor through volunteering or by offering up prayers for them (indeed, in the Church's tradition prayer and fasting always go together).

A first step toward living good lives in a capitalist order is to follow the five recommendations of all holy men and women: daily Mass, daily rosary, morning and evening offering, daily reflection on Scripture, and frequent confession. If all Catholics in capitalist economies practiced these norms, capitalism's inherent weaknesses would be less evident in society and its strengths would shine brighter.

WHAT'S OLD IS STILL NEW

We have focused mainly on consumer behavior, since that reflects the position of most readers, but moral capitalism also entails that *producers* engage in acts of sacrifice for the good of their workers.

This can include making the best effort to provide high wages and benefits that do not adversely affect overall the company's overall financial health. It could also include voluntarily adopting policies that allow for profit sharing and for corporate decision-making to be more widely dispersed among a firm's employees. For example, witness the Catholic Mondragon Corporation in Spain, the largest worker-owned cooperative in the world—though socialists like Noam Chomsky still complain that it exploits its workers because it seeks profits.[247]

Such proposals for employers could fill an entire other book, but we raise them here to make it clear that opposition to socialism does not entail support of the capitalism that John Paul II condemned: a system that lacks moral principles and a "strong juridical framework." Edward Feser, editor of *The Cambridge Companion to Hayek*, says capitalism is immoral when it turns into "fetishizing capitalism, of making market imperatives the governing principles to which all other aspects of social order are subordinate." He notes that even a stalwart critic of socialism like Hayek:

> explicitly allows for regulations to ensure safe working conditions, and for a safety net for those unable to provide adequate food, shelter, and health care for themselves. The Hayek who thought that the smallest tax increase is but the first step toward the Gulag exists only in the imaginations of uncharitable critics and simpleminded admirers.[248]

But carefully crafted economic policies by themselves are not enough to bring about authentic human fulfillment. Pope Leo insists that the only way to "restore" a fallen civilization is the "correction of morals"—transforming hearts and minds according to human and Christian virtue whose source is the life of God: grace. The pontiffs who have weighed in on—and against—socialism and Communism have tirelessly proclaimed that rejecting socialism is only part of the solution. The other part, as Pope Leo put it:

> The instruments which [the Church] employs are given to her by Jesus Christ himself for the very purpose of reaching the hearts of men, and drive their efficiency from God. They alone can reach the innermost heart and conscience, and bring men to act from a motive of duty, to control their passions and appetites, to love God and their fellow men with a love that is outstanding and of the highest degree and to break down courageously every barrier which blocks the way to virtue (*Rerum Novarum* 26).

There is no magic bullet. There is no quick fix—be it a bloody or unbloody revolution, or a set of policy platforms, or an accumulation of regulatory laws, that can make the world perfectly good. There is always the cross, and the task of evangelization that is ever the job of Christians. Though this is, properly speaking, apolitical, that doesn't mean the Church has no role guiding men and nations to the principles of right order—correcting and admonishing when, for instance, wicked solutions are proposed.

But the Church's mission to souls means that it fully exercises her role by lifting up and offering the food that never perishes, the food that leaves you never hungry again, the food that no political order can offer but is necessary for happiness in the order of this life, and more importantly, in the order of the life to come.

IT'S IMPORTANT TO REMEMBER . . .

- As a check against capitalism's potential to promote vices like consumerism and disordered desires, we must individually cultivate the virtue of temperance and corporately build a strong moral order.

- Even though wealth and free markets can be good things, as with all good things we need to fast from them periodically in order to keep our priorities in perspective.

- Our first identity is not that of laborer, producer, or consumer but disciple of Jesus Christ, working out our salvation through his Church.

APPENDIX:
WHAT ABOUT DISTRIBUTISM?

In our chapter on democratic socialism, we showed that in G.K. Chesterton and George Bernard Shaw's debate over socialism, Chesterton argued that socialism didn't really achieve its own goals. Socialists believed that wealth and property should be evenly distributed to all people, but Chesterton astutely pointed out:

> It is easy enough to say Property should be distributed, but who is, as it were, the subject of the verb? Who or what is to distribute? Now it is based on the idea that the central power which condescends to distribute will be permanently just, wise, sane, and representative of the conscience of the community which has created it. That is what we doubt.[249]

Chesterton believed that socialism kept property in the hands of a few government officials who then decided which people ought to receive it, and he saw such a system as inefficient at best and tyrannical at worst. However, Chesterton was just as critical of capitalism, which to him kept "productive property" (such as land and factory machinery) in the hands of a few business owners who lived in luxury while their employees endured crushing poverty. Chesterton did not want government to own capitalist property but instead to redistribute it to a greater number of people, so everyone else could benefit from it. He once quipped, "Too much capitalism does not mean too many capitalists but too few capitalists."

Chesterton, along with his friend and fellow Catholic author Hilaire Belloc and some other like-minded thinkers, wanted to resolve the debate between capitalism and socialism through a "third way" called *distributism* (also called *distributivism*). Instead of only a few businessmen or government officials owning productive property, they wanted as many people as possible to own this kind of property. Distributed widely enough throughout society, this property would then allow individuals and families to be self-sufficient and live without a capitalist paycheck or a socialist handout.

Did they hit upon a true "Catholic" economic system? After all, Chesterton and Belloc were both brilliant and beloved—even prophetic—Catholic lights of the last century who have many devoted followers today.

A complete assessment of distributism would require a book-length treatment, but here we will focus on three questions: 1) What is distributism? 2) *Must* Catholics be distributists? 3) *Should* Catholics be distributists?

WHAT IS DISTRIBUTISM?

Chesterton once summarized distributism this way: "three acres and a cow." The phrase had already been popular with British land reformers for decades, but in the first half of the twentieth century, distributists revived it to reinforce the idea that government should make sure all people have access to means that would make them self-sufficient. Belloc wrote, "A family possessed of the means of production—the simplest form of which is the possession of land and of the implements and capital for working the land—cannot be controlled by others."[250]

Belloc acknowledges that the members of such a family could still experience economic hardship if no one buys their goods, but since they at least have the means to be self-sufficient, they would never experience complete destitution. And distributists, then and now, admit that not everyone will turn to farming and make a living selling surplus food to others. Under distributism, some people would specialize their labor and produce other kinds of goods and services. But distributists believe that government should intervene in the market in order to prevent these economic actors from growing into large firms that crowd out smaller businesses and consequently concentrate ownership of the means of production into the hands of a few.

So, for example, instead a town having a shoe factory that sells thousands of shoes to customers near and far away, it should instead have only a few small shoemaker shops. Under such a scenario, prices for shoes would be high enough that a shoemaker would be guaranteed a livelihood he may not have received from his wage as a shoe factory employee.

Upon its creation in the 1920s, Chesterton's Distributist League argued for economic reforms along these lines, such as:[251]

- restraint of unjust competition;

- redistribution of property;

- creation of conditions favoring small ownership (such as by heavily taxing the sale of small companies to larger ones);

- extended ownership of industries that necessitated large-scale production;

- laws to protect distributed property;

- a return to the land; and

- encouragement of distributist principles by individuals.

One contemporary defense of distributism contrasts it with capitalism in this way: "Capitalism is that economic system where the private ownership of productive capital is separated from the work on that capital. Distributism is that economic system where the private ownership of productive capital is joined to the work on that capital."[252]

Distributists admit that capitalism does not prohibit the existence of small businesses (indeed, almost all large businesses start out small). But they believe that government should prevent businesses from growing to a size where the majority of workers are no longer owners of the company.

Distributists offer a variety of proposals to achieve this scenario, including resurrecting the concept of *guilds* to limit the number of people who could legally enter a trade. Restricting the number of people with specialized skills would keep their wages higher. Distributists also support laws aimed at making businesses "answerable to the local community they serve" by requiring local residency in order to operate a business in an area (which would put national and especially international corporations out of business).[253] David Cooney, the author of *Distributism Basics*, summarizes their goal in this way:

> All of this is based on the idea that a great multitude of small, privately owned businesses is better for society, and results in greater economic independence and freedom for the average citizen, than having large multi-national corporations employing tens of thousands of non-owner workers.[254]

MUST CATHOLICS BE DISTRIBUTISTS?

Some distributists describe their system as "Catholic economics" and even go so far as to say that Catholics have a moral duty to abandon capitalism and endorse distributism. But, as we showed earlier in this book, the Church has never said that capitalism is intrinsically evil, and Pope St. John

Paul II even said, "The Church's social doctrine is not a 'third way' between liberal capitalism and Marxist collectivism." [255] He also wrote in *Centesimus Annus*:

> The Church has no models to present; models that are real and truly effective can only arise within the framework of different historical situations, through the efforts of all those who responsibly confront concrete problems in all their social, economic, political and cultural aspects, as these interact with one another. For such a task the Church offers her social teaching as an *indispensable and ideal orientation,* a teaching which, as already mentioned, recognizes the positive value of the market and of enterprise, but which at the same time points out that these need to be oriented toward the common good.[256]

Some distributists cite exhortations in the Leonine papal encyclicals that call on society to make fundamental changes so that anyone can make a "family wage" capable of providing for even a large family. But these exhortations do not require Catholics to accept distributist proposals to achieve these goals over other ones aimed at the same goals, such as promoting job training for high-wage positions or efficient business practices that drive down the cost of goods in order to increase the purchasing power of a family's income.

Even defenders of distributism admit that their system is not exclusively Catholic in nature. Cooney says, "The philosophical basis for many distributist positions predates Christianity . . . its positions are an attempt to apply philosophical positions on economic and social structures in ways that are specifically compatible with the Catholic faith."[257]

Now, there is nothing wrong with taking older philosophies and making them applicable to the Faith (St. Thomas

Aquinas did just that with his synthesis of the writings of Aristotle). But it's incorrect to say that distributism is the only system of economic thought that is compatible with Catholicism.

As we noted earlier, "Catholic economics" is akin to "Catholic medicine." The deposit of faith does contain moral truths that tell us when a certain practice of either medicine or economics is evil. It also contains general truths that show us how to live in a way that is conducive to good health and in a way that is conducive to economic security. But just as our faith does not include systematic principles that tell us how to generate health and reduce illness (the science of medicine), it does not include systematic principles that tell us how to generate wealth and reduce poverty (the science of economics). To investigate and discover those principles in both cases, we have to turn (while still being guided by Catholic principles) to the empirical sciences.

Distributists, however, don't usually consider economics to be a science that studies the effects of allocating goods in order to satisfy demand. Cooney even criticizes capitalists for holding the view "that economics is a 'natural' science like chemistry or physics to which things like ethics and justice don't necessarily apply."[258] Fellow distributist John Medaille says, "Money—and economics—is not a 'neutral' science; bad ethics equals bad economics; bad morals equal bad money." Cooney even calls economics a "sub-field" of ethics and defines economics as being "about how people *should* [emphasis added] behave toward one another when engaged in transactions, no matter how trivial, to provide for their needs and wants."[259]

Since economics studies *people,* as a science it is more like the sciences of sociology or psychology than a "hard science" such as chemistry. Also, economists routinely study how ethical decisions affect economic transactions, but they would deny the distributist claim that the goal of economics is to create a normative philosophy to guide people's lives instead of a descriptive science that explains economic behaviors and outcomes.

Ethics is an important part of economics, and distributists should be commended for encouraging its inclusion in economic discussions. But economics and ethics belong to different, interdependent spheres; or as Pope Pius XI put it, "Economics and moral science each employs its own principles in its own sphere."[260] And distributists make the same error as socialists when they propose an economic system that relies on human beings always "being their best" (which rarely happens). Indeed, one of the benefits of capitalism is that it produces overall beneficial outcomes while assuming that people will act primarily out of their own self-interest.

Distributism's goals are laudable, but its methods contradict what we've learned from more than a century of economic studies. Although Catholics are free to embrace any distributist principles that don't contradict what the Church teaches, whether it is *prudent* for them to do that is a different question.

SHOULD CATHOLICS BE DISTRIBUTISTS?

We find there are many elements in distributist literature that are commendable, especially when it exposes excesses and deficiencies in capitalist economies. For example, monopolies that form when government provides preferential support to one company or hinders its competition can lead to economic exploitation and inefficient economies (this is often called "crony capitalism"). We also commend those who voluntarily choose to live a simpler lifestyle and seek an economic arrangement that allows them to achieve self-sufficiency apart from working for an established company. But we believe that distributism, in spite of the good elements it does possess, is not a viable model for modern economies.

Almost all professional economists (including Catholic ones) reject distributism as a complete economic model. In fact, among the twelve authors in a recent anthology in defense of distributism, not one is listed as holding advanced degrees in economics or is even identified as an economist.[261] This doesn't mean that distributism is wrong, but it does place upon defenders of distributism the burden of showing why their proposals are better than conventional economic models.

We believe that they have not met this burden, for a number reasons.

First, distributists fail to understand that their dramatic proposals have severe tradeoffs. Government cannot simply order by fiat that all companies remain small, pay a family wage, not lay off workers, and keep the price of goods low. Some of these goals end up conflicting with each other. Theologian David Deavel notes:

> Many distributists react to this information not by calculating the costs and benefits of such a predictable outcome, but instead by railing against "injustice." An "unjust" wage, for instance, is any salary that's insufficient to support a family—even a large one. So they wish to outlaw "unjust" wages. How would employers respond to such a move? Economics gives us the answer: they would either fire workers whose labor was not productive enough to justify such a wage, or else they would jack up prices to cover the extra cost. Who would pay those new, inflated prices? Ordinary workers, whose cost of living would soar—thus forcing another government-mandated rise in the "living wage." And so on, *ad infinitum*.[262]

Distributist policies would also drive up the price of goods and services so that "self-sufficient" families would struggle to afford many things they could once buy when they were employed. One of capitalism's benefits, in contrast, is that it has raised wages over time and helped make goods cheaper to produce. For example, in the year 1900, low wages and expensive goods meant the average family spent nearly half its income on food; but a century later, families were spending only 13 percent of their income on food.[263]

Second, when it comes to employment, security is not an absolute value. A slave has total "job security" (in a perverted sense of the term), yet hardly anyone would choose to be a fed, clothed, and housed slave than an unemployed free person. The fact is, nothing is secure in this world—including the distributist proposal for self-sufficiency.

Any number of things can ruin a small-scale farm, for example, and 20 percent of small businesses fail in their first year of operation (half fail in their first five years).[264] A recent study showed that only 19 percent of these businesses fail because other companies (both small and large ones) outcompeted them in the market. The most common reasons are a lack of demand for the service or product (42 percent), running out of money (29 percent), and mismanagement (23 percent).[265] Even the ideal distributist model cannot guarantee that such problems won't afflict the multitudinous small businesses that need to thrive under the distributist system.

Most modern people are also willing to trade the stress that comes with running their own company or farm for the stability that comes from working for an employer. Economist Thomas Woods says that the only thing preventing people from adopting the distributist proposal in their own lives is the difficulty of actually living out the proposal:

Practically anyone in the United States today who possesses the requisite knowledge and modest capital can acquire farmland and pursue the kind of self-sufficiency advocated by Belloc. Producing their own necessities and in possession of the means of production, such a family would be independent of employers or anyone else. They would probably also enjoy a standard of living so depressed and intolerable as to throw the rationality of the entire enterprise into question.[266]

A third reason distributism doesn't work is that the vast majority of the productive capital that exists today can't be distributed. Modern means of producing wealth are not tied to land or even machinery. For many people, the greatest piece of productive capital they own is their minds (Catholic philosopher Michael Novak once pointed out that the root of "capitalism" is *caput* or head). Some of the staunchest defenders of distributism can make a living with just a computer and a microphone because they are brilliant, and other people are willing to pay to hear their speeches and read their books. But you can't "distribute" the intellectual capital in their brains to those whose comparative lack of talent leads them to struggle.

Even when it comes to physical property that can be redistributed, doing so would quickly prevent companies from growing large enough to create such property in the first place. Why bother investing in equipment for a second factory if the government will just force you to make it a separate company co-owned by a small group of employees? Distributism's policy of redistributing property once companies become "too large" would be just as destructive as socialism's policy to redistribute earnings once a company becomes "too wealthy."

In addition, capitalism provides a way for people who aren't good at creating physical or intellectual property to offer their labor for a business venture and consequently give them a means not just to survive but even to flourish. There are millions of people who have worked for others, practiced thrift and modest living, and managed to save a small fortune to pass down to their heirs. A 2019 study from the National Bureau of Economic Research provides strong evidence that such a process of capital accumulation is still happening in the United States economy.[267]

No wonder that this is the means of economic mobility recommended by Pope Leo XIII in *Rerum Novarum*. The poor didn't need land or property (or machines or tools). What they needed were jobs and the ability to keep and save what they earned. What ends up hurting people who lack the will or the skill to start their own businesses are government restrictions that prevent or hinder the natural growth of a business and keep it from answering the needs of prospective employees who want to sell their labor in exchange for a relatively steady paycheck.

THREE "GIGS" AND A CAR?

The single biggest "distributive" experiment in modern history has been the cluster of innovation related to the so-called "gig economy." People are able to own and profit from their own means of production with everything from skilled freelance work to ride- and home-sharing although millions earn a living in that way, tens of millions more prefer the stability and predictability of salaried work.

The genius of modern enterprise is that it allows people with varied capacities and talents to combine their efforts into a productive venture that is bigger than the sum of their individual capital (be it physical or intellectual). Most people are better off in such collaborative enterprises than they would be if they were making direct use of their own resources through a self-owned business.

And this remains the biggest challenge for distributists: all capital isn't equally productive—and no capital is productive at all if it's not paired with the right persons and firms. Capitalism allows those who would thrive as entrepreneurs to do so, but distributism punishes those who would thrive working for entrepreneurs instead of being one.

These objections are not meant to be an exhaustive critique of distributism. We haven't addressed, for example, the difficulty in distributists' need for a paternalistic government to ensure that economies are "just." But even if that were possible (and we contend that it isn't), the Church urges instead that economies respect the principle of subsidiarity and local initiative. It highlights the subjective genius of the person over physical capital and has consistently praised the value of an economy in which old-fashioned labor, savings, and thrift provide hope and opportunity for the poor and working classes.

ENDNOTES

1   Mohamed Younis, "Four in 10 Americans Embrace Some Form of Socialism," Gallup, May 20, 2019, https://news.gallup.com/poll/257639/four-americans-embrace-form-socialism.aspx.

2   "Victims of Communism 2018 Annual Report," https://www.victimsofcommunism.org/2018-annual-report.

3   Glen H. Elder, *Children of the Great Depression: Social Change in Life Experience* (New York: Routledge, 2018), 44–45. Some median income losses reached as high as 64 percent, though anything above 40 percent usually required the sale of assets like homes to make up the difference.

4   John Steinbeck, *The Grapes of Wrath* (New York: Penguin, 2002), 348–349.

5   See Harvey Klehr, *The Heyday of American Communism: The Depression Decade* (New York, Basic Books, 1984).

6   Huey Long, "Every Man a King" in *American Political Speeches*, ed. Richard Beeman (New York: Penguin, 2012), 66.

7   Letter to Norman Thomas (September 25, 1951). See David Mikkelson, "Norman Thomas on Socialism" snopes.com (September 26, 2009), https://www.snopes.com/fact-check/norman-thomas-on-socialism/.

8   Rakesh Kochhar, "A Recovery No Better than the Recession Median Household Income, 2007 to 2011," Pew Research Center (2012), https://www.pewresearch.org/wp-content/uploads/sites/3/2012/09/median-household-incomes-2007–2011.pdf.

9   Joseph E. Stiglitz, "Of the 1 percent, by the 1 percent, for the 1 percent" *Vanity Fair* (May 2011), https://www.vanityfair.com/news/2011/05/top-one-percent-201105.

10 For a criticism Frank Newport, "Democrats More Positive About Socialism Than Capitalism," Gallup (August 13, 2018), https://news.gallup.com/poll/240725/democrats-positive-socialism-capitalism.aspx.

11 Keith A. Spencer, "Some millennials aren't saving for retirement because they don't think capitalism will exist by then," salon.com (March 18, 2018), https://www.salon.com/2018/03/18/some-millennials-arent-saving-for-retirement-because-they-do-not-think-capitalism-will-exist-by-then/.

12 "Tradinista Manifesto," https://tradinista.tumblr.com/manifesto.

13 David Bentley Hart, "Can We Please Relax About 'Socialism'?" *The New York Times* (April 27, 2019), https://www.nytimes.com/2019/04/27/opinion/sunday/socialism.html.

14 Dean Dettloff, "The Catholic Case for Communism," *America* (July 23, 2019), https://www.americamagazine.org/faith/2019/07/23/catholic-case-communism.

15 Derek Thompson, "Millennials' Political Views Don't Make Any Sense," The Atlantic (July 15, 2014), https://www.theatlantic.com/politics/archive/2014/07/millennials-economics-voting-clueless-kids-these-days/374427/.

16 Frank Newport, "Democrats More Positive About Socialism Than Capitalism," Gallup (August 13, 2018), https://news.gallup.com/poll/240725/democrats-positive-socialism-capitalism.aspx.

17 Derek Thompson, "Millennials' Political Views Don't Make Any Sense," The Atlantic (July 15, 2014), https://www.theatlantic.com/politics/archive/2014/07/millennials-economics-voting-clueless-kids-these-days/374427/.

18 David Bentley Hart, "Can We Please Relax About 'Socialism'?" *The New York Times* (April 27, 2019), https://www.nytimes.com/2019/04/27/opinion/sunday/socialism.html.

19 William Bradford, "Of Plymouth Plantation," *The English Literatures of America: 1500–1800*, eds. Myra Jehlen and Michael Warner (New York: Routledge, 1997), 187.

20 *Politics*, II.3.

21 Matthew Sheffield, "20 percent of Americans can't define 'socialism' even as it's become the focus of 2020," *The Hill* (May 31, 2019), https://thehill.com/hilltv/what-americas-thinking/446377-20-percent-of-americans-cant-define-socialism-even-as-its.

22 Bhaskar Sunkara, "End Private Property, Not Kenny Loggins," *Jacobin* (February, 2016), https://jacobinmag.com/2016/02/socialism-marxism-private-property-person-lennon-imagine-kenny-loggins.

23 Karl Marx and Friedrich Engels, *Manifesto of the Communist Party* (1848), Chapter II, https://www.marxists.org/archive/marx/works/1848/communist-manifesto/ch02.htm.

24 Jeff Stein, "9 questions about the Democratic Socialists of America you were too embarrassed to ask," *Vox* (August 5, 2017), https://www.vox.com/policy-and-politics/2017/8/5/15930786/dsa-socialists-convention-national.

25 Danny Katch, *Socialism . . . Seriously: A Brief Guide to Human Liberation* (Chicago: Haymarket Books, 2015), 76.

26 George Ritzer, *Essentials of Sociology* (Los Angeles: Sage Publications, 2016), 289.

27 Karl Marx and Friedrich Engels, *Manifesto of the Communist Party* (1848), Chapter II, https://www.marxists.org/archive/marx/works/1848/communist-manifesto/ch02.htm.

28 Friedrich Engels, *Origin of the Family, Private Property, and the State* (1884), https://www.marxists.org/archive/marx/works/download/pdf/origin_family.pdf.

29 https://www.worldsocialism.org/english/what-socialism.

30 Fritz Oerter, "Our Speakers in the Anti-Marxist Struggle," in *The Third Reich Sourcebook*, eds. Anson Rabinbach and Sander L. Gilman (Los Angeles, CA: University of California Press, 2013), 34.

31 Ian Kershaw, *Hitler: A Biography* (New York: W.W. Norton, 2008), 270.

32 Etienne Cabet's, *Voyage to Icaria* (1842), https://www.marxists.org/subject/utopian/cabet/icarus.htm.

33 Pope Paul VI acknowledged the peril of those who avoid realistic solutions in favor of unrealistic utopianism when he said, "The appeal to a utopia is often a convenient excuse for those who wish to escape from concrete tasks in order to take refuge in an imaginary world. To live in a hypothetical future is a facile alibi for rejecting immediate responsibilities."

34 A similar point is made in Justin Haskins, *Socialism Is Evil: The Moral Case Against Marx's Radical Dream* (Boston: The Henry Dearborn Institute for Liberty, 2018), 36.

35 Karl Marx, *The German Ideology* (1845), https://www.marxists.org/archive/marx/works/1845/german-ideology/ch01a.htm.

36 F.A. Hayek, "The Use of Knowledge in Society," *The American Economic Review*, Vol. 35, No. 4. (September 1945), 522.

37 John F. Burns, "Soviet Food Shortages: Grumbling And Excuses," *The New York Times* (January 15, 1982), https://www.nytimes.com/1982/01/15/world/soviet-food-shortages-grumbling-and-excuses.html.

38 Melford E. Spiro, "Utopia and Its Discontents: The Kibbutz and Its Historical Vicissitudes," *American Anthropologist*, Vol. 106, No. 3 (September 2004), 556–568.

39 As one historian puts it, "communities dwindled and dissolved due to lack of able-bodied, hard-working members. Each time they experienced a setback, they started anew, until finally there were no more young members—and there was no more fresh energy—to continue the community." Jyotsna Sreenivasan, *Utopias in American History* (Santa Barbara: ABC-CLIO, 2008), 188.

40 Frank Newport, "The Meaning of 'Socialism' to Americans Today," *Gallup* (October 4, 2018), https://news.gallup.com/opinion/polling-matters/243362/meaning-socialism-americans-today.aspx.

41 Friedrich Engels, "The Principles of Communism" (1847), https://www.marxists.org/archive/marx/works/1847/11/prin-com.htm.

42 Shaw said that Chesterton's crimes were those "of imagination and humor, not of malice," while Chesterton said of Shaw, "It is necessary to disagree with him

as much as I do in order to admire him as much as I do," https://www.jstor.org/
stable/40681668?seq=1#page_scan_tab_contents.

43   Chesterton, following a model proposed by fellow Catholic author Hilaire Belloc,
argued that it was not *wealth* that should be re-distributed among people but the
means to produce wealth. This "distributism" would take power away from governments
and factories and return it to individual families who could produce their own
livelihoods. That's why Chesterton is reported to have said, "The problem with
capitalism is not that there are too many Capitalists, but that there are too few."
(Chesterton even blamed capitalism for "killing the family" because it drew men
away from the home to work in factories and kept them from being self-sufficient.).

44   Dorothy Day, "Communists Communicate," *The Catholic Worker* (January 1937),
5, https://www.catholicworker.org/dorothyday/articles/527.html. Cited in Stephen
Beale, "The Dorothy Day Few of Us Know," *Crisis* (March 19, 2013), https://www.
crisismagazine.com/2013/the-dorothy-day-few-of-us-know.

45   "We believe that social security legislation, now billed as a great victory for the poor
and for the worker, is a great defeat for Christianity. It is an acceptance of the idea
of force and compulsion. It is an acceptance of Cain's statement, on the part of the
employer. 'Am I my brother's keeper?' Since the employer can never be trusted to
give a family wage, nor take care of the worker as he takes care of his machine when
it is idle, the state must enter in and compel help on his part." Dorothy Day, "On
Pilgrimage," *The Catholic Worker* (January 1973) 2, 6, https://www.catholicworker.
org/dorothyday/articles/150.pdf. "Actually if the State, City, and the whole secular
world with its 'inspector generals' and bureaucracies did not demand our conformity
to such insane standards of luxury, Holy Mother the Church would not have to be
pleading for funds for schools, and books, and buses, and health and welfare aids.
(As St. Hilary wrote a thousand (or a few days) ago, 'The less we ask of Caesar, the
less we will have to render to Caesar.)'" Dorothy Day, "More About Holy Poverty.
Which Is Voluntary Poverty," *The Catholic Worker* (February 1945) 1-2, https://www.
catholicworker.org/dorothyday/articles/527.html.

46   Maurice Isserman, *The Other American: The Life Of Michael Harrington* (New York:
PublicAffairs, 2000), 70.

47   Michael Harrington, *Socialism: Past and Future* (New York: Little, Brown & Co.,
1989), 197.

48   "About us," *Democratic Socialists of America*, https://www.dsausa.org/about-us/.

49   Danielle Kurtzleben, "Getting To Know The DSA," *National Public Radio* (July 19,
2018), https://www.npr.org/2018/07/19/630394669/getting-to-know-the-dsa.

50   Neal Meyer, "What is Democratic Socialism," *Jacobin* (July 2018), https://
jacobinmag.com/2018/07/democratic-socialism-bernie-sanders-social-democracy-
alexandria-ocasio-cortez.

51   Friedrich Engels, *Origin of the Family, Private Property, and the State* (1884), https://
www.marxists.org/archive/marx/works/download/pdf/origin_family.pdf.

52   Lillian Cicerchia laments that, when it comes to abortion, Catholic hospitals aren't
"compelled to offer the service" though she hopes that through government-backed
universal health care, "The waiting periods, the counseling, the religious exemptions, the
feticide laws, [would] all have to go." Lillian Cicerchia, "What Medicare for All Means
for Abortion Rights," *Jacobin* (January 18, 2019), https://www.jacobinmag.com/2019/01/
medicare-for-all-abortion-hyde-trap-laws-reproductive-justice.

53   Rationing of palliative care leading people to feel that assisted suicide is the only
way to treat their pain has become a problem in Canada's nationalized health care
program. See Peter Stockland, "Assisted dying was supposed to be an option. To
some patients, it looks like the only one," *Maclean's* (June 22, 2018), https://www.
macleans.ca/society/assisted-dying-was-supposed-to-be-an-option-to-some-
patients-it-looks-like-the-only-one/.

54   Neal Meyer, "What is Democratic Socialism," *Jacobin* (July 2018), https://

jacobinmag.com/2018/07/democratic-socialism-bernie-sanders-social-democracy-alexandria-ocasio-cortez.

55   David Bentley Hart, "Can We Please Relax About 'Socialism'?" *The New York Times* (April 27, 2019), https://www.nytimes.com/2019/04/27/opinion/sunday/socialism.html.

56   Jose Mena, "The Catholic turn to socialism is something to celebrate," *Catholic Herald* (May 30, 2019), https://catholicherald.co.uk/commentandblogs/2019/05/30/the-catholic-turn-to-socialism-is-something-to-celebrate/.

57   Barbara Ehrenreich, *Nickel and Dimed: On (Not) Getting By in America* (New York: Henry Holt and Company, 2001), 68.

58   Erika Christakis, "Is Paul Ryan's Budget 'Un-Christian'?" *Time Magazine*, August 14, 2012, http://ideas.time.com/2012/08/14/why-paul-ryans- budget-unchristian/.

59   According to economist Lawrence Reed, "The fact is, one can scour the scriptures with a fine-tooth comb and find nary a word from Jesus that endorses the forcible redistribution of wealth by political authorities. None, period." Lawrence Reed, *Render Unto Caesar: Was Jesus a Socialist?* (Atlanta, GA: Foundation for Economic Education, 2015), Kindle edition.

60   "By and large, only the dishonorable rich, the dishonorable nonelites, and those beyond the pale of public opinion (such as city elites, governors, regional kings) could accumulate wealth with impunity. This they did in a number of ways, notably by trading, tax collecting, and money lending. . . . In the first century [these methods] would all be considered dishonorable and immoral forms of usury." Bruce Malina, *The New Testament World: Insights from Cultural Anthropology* (Louisville, KY: Westminster John Knox Press, 2001), 104–105.

61   Craig Blomberg, "Neither Capitalism nor Socialism: A Biblical Theology of Economics," *Journal of Markets & Morality*, Vol. 15 No. 1 (Spring 2012), 211.

62   Justin Martyr wrote to the Roman Emperor "[W]e who valued above all things the acquisition of wealth and possessions, now bring what we have into a common stock, and communicate to every one in need . . ." (*First Apology*, 14). Lucian had a more cynical view saying in *The Passing of Peregrinus*, "they despise all things indiscriminately and consider them common property, receiving such doctrines traditionally without any definite evidence. So if any charlatan and trickster, able to profit by occasions, comes among them, he quickly acquires sudden wealth by imposing upon simple folk."

63   Julian the Apostate, *Letter to Arsacius.*

64   David Bentley Hart, "Can We Please Relax About 'Socialism'?" *The New York Times* (April 27, 2019), https://www.nytimes.com/2019/04/27/opinion/sunday/socialism.html.

65   *Homily II on Eutropius.*

66   *Serf* comes from the Latin *servus*, which means "slave" and while serfdom is considered on par with slavery today, in the medieval world serfdom was considered a moral improvement to Roman slavery. In the time of Jesus a slave was not a person but rather, as one historian notes, "a slave was res, a thing, property, an object . . . wounding or killing a slave was usually counted as damage to property."

67   This can be seen in the writings of figures like Henri Saint-Simon and Robert Owens. For precursors see J.C. Davis *Utopia and the Ideal Society: A Study of English Utopian Writing, 1516–1700* (1983).

68   Karl Marx and Friedrich Engels, *Manifesto of the Communist Party* (1848), https://www.marxists.org/archive/marx/works/1848/communist-manifesto/ch04.htm.

69   Tim Harford, "Is this the most influential work in the history of capitalism?" BBC (October 23, 2017), https://www.bbc.com/news/business-41582244.

70   Mark Dodgson & David Gann, *Innovation: A Very Short Introduction* (New York: Oxford University Press, 2010), 9.

71   Peter R. Cox, *Demography*, 5th ed. (Cambridge: Cambridge University Press, 1976), 195.

72   Charles Dickens, *Hard Times*, ed. Graham Law (Toronto: Broadview Press, 2000), 60.

73   Friedrich Engels, "The Great Towns," (1845), https://www.marxists.org/archive/marx/works/1845/condition-working-class/ch04.htm.

ENDNOTES

74 Modern research refutes this. See for example Peter H. Lindert and Jeffrey G. Williamson, "English Workers' Living Standards during the Industrial Revolution: A New Look," *The Economic History Review New Series*, Vol. 36, No. 1 (February 1983), 20–25.

75 ". . . and as for the other men, who worked in tank rooms full of steam, and in some of which there were open vats near the level of the floor, their peculiar trouble was that they fell into the vats; and when they were fished out, there was never enough of them left to be worth exhibiting—sometimes they would be overlooked for days, till all but the bones of them had gone out to the world as Durham's Pure Leaf Lard!" Upton Sinclair, *The Jungle* (New York: Doubleday, Page & Company, 1906), 117.

76 Earle Labor, *Jack London: An American Life* (New York: Farrar, Straus, and Giroux, 2013), 230.

77 Carl Jensen, *Stories that Changed America: Muckrakers of the 20ᵗʰ Century* (New York, Seven Stories Press, 2000), 56.

78 Friedrich Engels, *The Condition of the Working Class in England* (New York: Oxford University Press, 1999), 127.

79 "He receives a certificate from society that he has furnished such-and-such an amount of labor (after deducting his labor for the common funds); and with this certificate, he draws from the social stock of means of consumption as much as the same amount of labor cost. The same amount of labor which he has given to society in one form, he receives back in another." Karl Marx, *Critique of the Gotha Programme* (1875), https://www.marxists.org/archive/marx/works/1875/gotha/.

80 These include the 1886 Haymarket riot and the radical anarchist Paris commune that ruled the city during the Spring of 1871.

81 Jean Jacques Rousseau, "On the Origin of the Inequality of Mankind: The Second Part" (1754), https://www.marxists.org/reference/subject/economics/rousseau/inequality/ch02.htm.

82 P.J. Proudhon, *Qu'est-ce que la Propriété?, ou, recherches sur le principe du droit et du Gouvernement* (Paris, 1840), 2.

83 Karl Marx, "Letter to J. B. Schweizer 'On Proudhon'" (1865), https://www.marxists.org/archive/marx/works/1865/letters/65_01_24.htm.

84 "That the civil government should at its option intrude into and exercise intimate control over the family and the household is a great and pernicious error. True, if a family finds itself in exceeding distress, utterly deprived of the counsel of friends, and without any prospect of extricating itself, it is right that extreme necessity be met by public aid, since each family is a part of the commonwealth" (*Rerum Novarum* 14).

85 *De Finibus*, Book III.

86 Marissa Fessenden, "Making a Sandwich from Scratch Took This Man Six Months," *Smithsonian Magazine* (September 18, 2015), https://www.smithsonianmag.com/smart-news/making-sandwich-scratch-took-man-six-months-180956674/.

87 Adam Smith, *An Inquiry Into the Nature and Causes of the Wealth of Nations*, Vol. 2 (London, William Clowes and Sons, 1835), 55.

88 Clarence Darrow, *The Essential Words and Writings of Clarence Darrow*, eds. Edward J. Larson and Jack Marshall (New York: Random House, 2007), 236.

89 Jean-Jacques Rousseau, *Emile or On Education*, trans. Allan Bloom (USA: Basic Books, 1979), 237.

90 Stephen White, *Communism and its Collapse* (New York: Routledge, 2001), 3.

91 Peter Gahan, *Bernard Shaw and Beatrice Webb on Poverty and Equality in the Modern World, 1905–1914* (Palgrave Macmillan, 2017), 106.

92 "Dialog of Catherine of Siena," 4.2.5, https://www.ccel.org/ccel/catherine/dialog.iv.ii.vii.html.

93 Paul Lafargue, *The Right to be Lazy* (1883), https://www.marxists.org/archive/lafargue/1883/lazy/ch01.htm.

94 "Tradinista Manifesto," https://tradinista.tumblr.com/manifesto.

95 Mark Schmitt, "The case for helping the 'unwilling to work,'" *Vox* (February 20,

2019), https://www.vox.com/polyarchy/2019/2/20/18233515/unwilling-to-work-jobs-employment-aoc-green-new-deal.

96   Aaron Bastani, *Fully Automated Luxury Communism* (New York, Verso, 2019).

97   "What is Democratic Socialism?" https://www.dsausa.org/about-us/what-is-democratic-socialism/. Other writers claim that once technology advances enough we will be like characters in the *Star Trek* series who do not worry about acquiring scare resources and focus on leisure and exploration. Of course, even people on the Enterprise had jobs and some of them seemed quite demanding (not to mention hazardous for the red shirted crew members).

98   Karl Marx, "The Victory of the Counter-Revolution in Vienna" (1848), https://www.marxists.org/archive/marx/works/1848/11/06.htm.

99   Abraham Ascher, *The Revolution of 1905: A Short History* (Stanford: Stanford University Press, 2004), 5.

100   Karl Marx, *Critique of the Gotha Programme* (1875), https://www.marxists.org/archive/marx/works/1875/gotha/ch01.htm.

101   Vladimir Lenin, *The State and Revolution* (1917), https://www.marxists.org/archive/lenin/works/1917/staterev/ch05.htm.

102   Myles J. Kelleher, *Social Problems in a Free Society: Myths, Absurdities, and Realities* (Lanham, MD: University Press of America, 2004), 60. The origin of the nail factory example can be traced all the way back to Krokodil, a satirical Russian magazine, that featured a cartoon depicting a proud factory manager hoisting a single giant nail as evidence of his plant's successful output.

103   "Throughout the Soviet Union, the direct loss of life due to the famine and associated hunger and disease was likely to be six to eight million. Three to five million of this number died in Ukraine and in the heavily Ukraine-populated northern Kuban, among the richest grain producing areas of Europe. The Ukrainian word Holodomor derives from a combination of the word for hunger, *holod*, and *mor*, to exterminate or eliminate." Norman M. Naimark, *Stalin's Genocides* (Princeton: Princeton University Press, 2010), 70.

104   Robert Conquest, *The Harvest of Sorrow: Soviet Collectivization and the Terror-Famine* (New York: Oxford University Press, 1986), 257.

105   Marcel H. Van Herpen, *Putin's Propaganda Machine: Soft Power and Russian Foreign Policy* (Lanham, MD: Rowan and Littlefield, 2016), 68.

106   Walter Duranty, *The New York Times*, August 23, 1933. In 2003 Mark von Hagen, a Columbia University history professor, hired by the *Times* to review Duranty's work, said, "For the sake of *The New York Times'* honor, they should take the prize away." "N.Y. Times urged to rescind 1932 Pulitzer" (October 22, 2003), https://usatoday30.usatoday.com/news/nation/2003-10-22-ny-times-pulitzer_x.htm.

107   Dana G. Dalrymple, "The Soviet Famine of 1932–1934," Soviet Studies, Vol. 15, No. 3 (January 1964), 250–284.

108   George Orwell, "Politics and the English Language" (1968), https://faculty.washington.edu/rsoder/EDLPS579/HonorsOrwellPoliticsEnglishLanguage.pdf.

109   Jose Mena, "The Catholic turn to socialism is something to celebrate," *Catholic Herald* (May 30, 2019), https://catholicherald.co.uk/.commentandblogs/2019/05/30/the-catholic-turn-to-socialism-is-something-to-celebrate/.

110   Vladimir Lenin, "The Attitude of the Workers' Party to Religion" (1909), https://www.marxists.org/archive/lenin/works/1909/may/13.htm.

111   Patrick McNamara, *A Catholic Cold War: Edmund A. Walsh, S.J., and the Politics of American Anticommunism* (New York: Fordham University Press, 2005), 28.

112   Kent R. Hill, *The Soviet Union on the Brink: An Inside Look at Christianity & Glasnost* (Portland, OR: Multnomah, 1991), 83.

113   Katherine Bliss Eaton, *Daily Life in the Soviet Union* (Westport, CT: Greenwood Press, 2004), 289.

114   Brianne Jacobs, "Yes, democratic socialism is compatible with Catholic social

teaching," *America* (October 1, 2018), https://www.americamagazine.org/politics-society/2018/10/01/yes-democratic-socialism-compatible-catholic-social-teaching.

115 Karl Marx and Friedrich Engels, *Manifesto of the Communist Party* (1848), chapter II, https://www.marxists.org/archive/marx/works/1848/communist-manifesto/ch02.htm.

116 Leon Trotsky, *The Revolution Betrayed* (1936), https://www.marxists.org/archive/trotsky/1936/revbet/ch07.htm.

117 Philip Boobyer, *The Stalin Era* (New York: Routledge, 2000), 154.

118 "The Feminists vs. The Institution of Marriage," *Sisterhood is Powerful*, ed. Robin Morgan (New York: Random House, 1970), 537.

119 Cited in John Hirschauer, "Candace Bushnell's Childless Misery," *National Review* (July 31, 2019), https://www.nationalreview.com/2019/07/candace-bushnells-childless-misery/.

120 Rosemarie Ho, "Want to Dismantle Capitalism? Abolish the Family," *The Nation* (May 16, 2019), https://www.thenation.com/article/want-to-dismantle-capitalism-abolish-the-family/.

121 John O. Koehler, *Stasi: The Untold Story Of The East German Secret Police* (Boulder, CO: Westview Press, 1999), 9.

122 Mao Zedong, "Problems of War and Strategy" (1938), *Selected Works of Mao Tse-tung: Vol. II*, https://www.marxists.org/reference/archive/mao/selected-works/volume-2/mswv2_12.htm#p6.

123 Gabe T. Wang, *China and the Taiwan Issue: Impending War at Taiwan Strait* (Lanham, MD: University Press of America, 2006), 56–57.

124 Neil C. Hughes, *China's Economic Challenge: Smashing the Iron Rice Bowl* (New York: Routledge, 2015), 7.

125 Yang Jisheng, *Tombstone: The Great Chinese Famine, 1958–1962* (New York: Farrar, Straus, and Giroux, 2012), 3.

126 Ibid, 289.

127 Ibid, 40.

128 Ibid, 322.

129 Mao Zedong, "Speeches At The Second Session Of The Eighth Party Congress" (1958), https://www.marxists.org/reference/archive/mao/selected-works/volume-8/mswv8_10.htm.

130 "North Korea," *CIA World Factbook*, https://www.cia.gov/library/publications/the-world-factbook/geos/kn.html. See also David Wharton, "'Peace Village,' a fake city just outside the DMZ, serves as metaphor for North Korean athletes at the Olympics" *Los Angeles Times* (February 17, 2018), https://www.latimes.com/sports/olympics/la-sp-olympics-north-korea-mystery-20180217-story.html.

131 Chloe Pfeiffer and Elena Holodny, "14 fascinating facts about North Korea," *Business Insider* (April 18, 2017), https://www.businessinsider.com/weird-facts-about-north-korea-2017-4.

132 Chris Coney, "East Asia: History and Economic Development," *Encyclopedia of the Developing World*, Vol., 1 ed. Thomas M. Leonard (New York: Routledge, 2006), 511.

133 A transcript of the press conference says, "Question from Shabtai Gold at DPA: Can I clarify something earlier, you said the height and weight in DPRK is similar to that of other Asian countries, did I hear you right? Dr. Chan: I said what I saw in Pangung might not be representative for the entire country, but that is what I saw in the capital. Of course, one thing I recognized is that walking is quite well observed in that country, and I suggest that is why I didn't see many obese people. And if you look at me I am also an Asian, I am pretty short by Asian standards, so when I compare to most of the people I saw on the street, I can only make a very broad comparison. But mind you, as I said, now in Asian countries, because of affluence and intake of food we are seeing obesity which I don't see in DPRK." Transcript of press briefing at WHO headquarters, Geneva Dr. Margaret Chan, WHO Director-General (April 30, 2010), https://www.who.int/mediacentre/news/releases/2010/20100430_chan_press_

transcript.pdf. And while Chan was born in Hong Kong, her later education in Canada and Harvard certainly qualify her to be a "western intellectual" who whitewashes the impact of socialism on the health of North Korean people.

134 Gustavo Gutierrez, *A Theology of Liberation* (Maryknoll, NY: Orbis Books, 1988), 157.

135 The CDF rebuked the idea that evil can be localized "principally or uniquely in bad social, political, or economic 'structures' as though all other evils came from them so that the creation of the 'new man' would depend on the establishment of different economic and socio-political structures" (15).

136 *Instruction on Certain Aspects of the "Theology of Liberation,"* 7.

137 Mary Anastasia O'Grady, "Counting Castro's Victims," *The Wall Street Journal* (December 30, 2005), https://www.wsj.com/articles/SB113590852154334404.

138 "The intention of Cuba's new leaders was deviously clear. Carlos Franqui, editor of the official newspaper *Revolución*, has reported that in a speech of May 18, 1962 at State Security offices in Havana, Ché Guevara stated: 'It is logical that in times of excessive tension we cannot proceed weakly. We have imprisoned many people without knowing for sure if they were guilty. At the Sierra Maestra, we executed many people by firing squad without knowing if they were fully guilty. At times, the Revolution cannot stop to conduct much investigation; it has the obligation to triumph.'" María C. Werlau, "Ché Guevara's Forgotten Victims," *Free Society Project* (2011), http://cubaarchive.org/home/images/stories/che-guevara_interior-pages_en_final.pdf. University students who love to sport Ché paraphernalia would be shocked to know that people who identified as homosexual were considered a byproduct of "bourgeoisie decadence" that needed to be imprisoned and forced into hard labor. Andrea Pitzer, *One Long Night: A Global History of Concentration Camps* (New York: Little, Brown, and Company, 2018), 278–279.

139 These included not just conscientious objectors and minority religious groups like Jehovah's Witnesses, but also homosexuals whose sexual behavior was seen as a bourgeoisie defect. See Ian Lumsden, *Machos Maricones & Gays: Cuba and Homosexuality* (Philadelphia, PA: Temple University Press, 1996), 66–71.

140 Eliana Cardsos and Ann Helwege, *Cuba After Communism* (Boston, MA: Massachusetts Institute of Technology, 1992), 42. While the authors' predictions of Cuba's collapse or renouncement of socialism by the 21st century were incorrect, the book's descriptions of life in Cuba under Castro during the end of the Cold War are still a valuable resource.

141 The article also mentions the U.S. trade embargo as a reason for Cuba's shortages, but that doesn't explain why the nation fails to produce sufficient domestic foodstuffs that do not need to be imported in large quantities (though the collapse of its major trading partner Venezuela may also be a factor in Cuba's shortages). Sarah Marsh and Nelson Acosta, "Cuba to ration more products due to economic crisis, U.S. sanctions," *Reuters* (May 10, 2019), https://www.reuters.com/article/us-cuba-economy/cuba-to-ration-more-products-due-to-economic-crisis-u-s-sanctions-idUSKCN1SG2HA.

142 Joe Lamar, "For Cubans, the struggle to supplement meager rations is a consuming obsession," *The Guardian* (April 24, 2015), https://www.theguardian.com/world/2015/apr/24/cubans-food-struggle-rations-consuming-obsession.

143 Katherine Hirschfeld, "Re-examining the Cuban Health Care System: Towards a Qualitative Critique," *Cuban Affairs*, Vol. 2, Issue 3 (July 2007), 7.

144 Gilbert Berdine, Vincent Geloso, and Benjamin Powell "Cuban infant mortality and longevity: health care or repression?" *Health Policy and Planning*, Vol. 33, Issue 6, (July 2018) 755–757.

145 See Yvonne Conde, *Operation Pedro Pan: The Untold Exodus of 14,048 Cuban Children* (New York: Routledge, 1999).

146 Part of this rise in Cuban asylum claims comes from the reversal of previous immigration policies that allowed Cubans who reached American shores to remain

ENDNOTES

in the country to pursue citizenship. See Santiago Perez, "Cuban Migrants Are Thwarted in Mexico by New Asylum Rules," *The Wall Street Journal* (August 2, 2019), https://www.wsj.com/articles/cuban-migrants-are-thwarted-in-mexico-by-new-asylum-rules-11564738202.

147 "Nikita Khrushchev: Speech on Decolonization," *The Cold War: Interpreting Conflict through Primary Documents*, Vol. 2, ed. Priscilla Roberts (Santa Barbara, CA: ABC-CLIO, 2019), 507.

148 William Taubman, *Khrushchev: The Man and His Era* (New York: W.W. Norton & Company Inc., 2003), 657. Most accounts say Khrushchev banged his shoe on his desk, but *New York Times* reporter James Feron claims that he never saw Khrushchev bang the shoe, but only menacingly wave it in the air.

149 Ibid., 427.

150 B.R. Shenoy, "East and West Berlin: A Study in Free vs. Controlled Economy" (August 15, 1960), https://www.libertarianism.org/publications/essays/east-west-berlin-study-free-vs-controlled-economy.

151 "It was this systematic lowering of unnecessarily high taxes that produced the German 'economic miracle.'" Jude Wanniski, "Taxes, Revenues, and the 'Laffer Curve,'" *The Politics of American Economic Policy Making*, 2nd edition, ed. Paul Peretz (New York, Routledge, 2015), 232.

152 And, to add insult to injury, the East German socialist economy required people to stay on a waiting list for *ten years* before they could buy one! Neil Harris, *European Business* (London: Macmillan Press, 1996), 117.

153 B.R. Shenoy, "East and West Berlin: A Study in Free vs. Controlled Economy" (August 15, 1960), https://www.libertarianism.org/publications/essays/east-west-berlin-study-free-vs-controlled-economy.

154 See Randal Bytwerk, "German Propaganda Archive," https://research.calvin.edu/german-propaganda-archive/notiz3.htm. Bytwerk lists his source as: *Wer die Deutsche Demokratische Republik verläßt, stellt sich auf die Seite der Kriegstreiber, Notizbuch des Agitators* (Agitator's Notebook), published by the Socialist Unity Party's Agitation Department, Berlin District, November 1955. See also Jim Willis, *Daily Life Behind the Iron Curtain* (Santa Barbara, CA: ABC-CLIO, 2013), 40.

155 Bernard Brien, *Blessed Jerzy Popieluszko: Truth versus Totalitarianism*, trans. Michael J. Miller (San Francisco: Ignatius Press, 2016), 110.

156 Socialist leaders often rely on the raw sale of natural resources on the open (world) market to get cash to buy foodstuffs and other goods that their deformed economies cannot produce. When the world price of such a resource, like oil, plummets, terrible misery can ensue when the government could no longer import food or medicine. This is what happened in Venezuela as we note in chapter nineteen.

157 Mary Elise Sarotte, *The Collapse: The Accidental Opening of the Berlin Wall* (New York: Basic Books, 2014), 117–118.

158 Kim Kelly, "What 'Capitalism' Is and How It Affects People" *Teen Vogue* (April 11, 2018), https://www.teenvogue.com/story/what-capitalism-is.

159 Zack Beauchamp, "Steven Pinker explains how capitalism is killing war," *Vox* (June 4, 2015), https://www.vox.com/2015/6/4/8725775/pinker-capitalism.

160 Adam Smith, *The Theory of Moral Sentiments* (New York: Penguin Books, 2009), Kindle edition.

161 Jay Richards, *Money, Greed, and God: Why Capitalism is the Solution and Not the Problem* (New York: HarperCollins, 2009), 123.

162 ST. II-II Q. 26 A4.

163 "[W]e reject the 'greed principle' that motivates so many in the capitalistic world. Capitalism relies solely on the idea that people work for profits." Tony Campolo, *Letters to a Young Evangelical* (New York: Basic Books, 2006), 142.

164 Joseph Alois Schumpeter, *Capitalism, socialism, and democracy* (New York: Harper Perennial, 1950), 67.

165 A similar phenomenon occurs under "crony capitalism" when failing businesses are propped up by government spending, which distorts free-market exchanges since government has almost endless abilities to raise revenues and continue this kind of spending through taxation or borrowing.

166 The modern robber-baron myth comes from Matthew Josephson's 1934 book *The Robber Barons*. It was a best-seller in an economically depressed United States eager to pain the rich as villains and markets as their chief weapon against the poor.

167 Vanderbilt started his first ferry service with a $100 loan from his mother. It later grew into the People's Line which competed at the time with a state-funded monopoly called the Hudson River Steamboat Association controlled ferry travel into New York and kept prices artificially high. Through ingenious business plans, Vanderbilt was able to offer lower prices along with more reliable service. At one point, he was able to give away free tickets because he made more than enough profit by selling food and drink on his boats. Eventually the other steamboat operators paid Vanderbilt not to compete with them, and it was this act that earned him the title of "Robber Barron" among later biographers like Matthew Josephson.

168 Ron Chernow, *Titan: The Life of John D. Rockefeller, Sr.* (New York: Random House, 2004), 257.

169 Ibid., 487.

170 Ché Guevara, "Socialism and man in Cuba" (1965), https://www.marxists.org/archive/guevara/1965/03/man-socialism.htm.

171 Abigail Marsh, "Could A More Individualistic World Also Be A More Altruistic One?" *National Public Radio* (February 5, 2018), https://www.npr.org/sections/13.7/2018/02/05/581873428/could-a-more-individualistic-world-also-be-a-more-altruistic-one.

172 Ibid., 120.

173 Adam Smith, *An Inquiry Into the Nature and Causes of the Wealth of Nations*, Vol. 2 (London, William Clowes and Sons, 1835), 54.

174 "Participation At The Second World Meeting Of Popular Movements Address Of The Holy Father" (July 9, 2015), http://w2.vatican.va/content/francesco/en/speeches/2015/july/documents/papa-francesco_20150709_bolivia-movimenti-popolari.html.

175 William F. Buckley credits the quote to early *National Review* collaborator Willi Schlamm. For more, see https://quoteinvestigator.com/2016/06/30/trouble/#return-note-13985-5.

176 "Visit To The Joint Session Of The United States Congress Address Of The Holy Father" (September 24, 2015), http://w2.vatican.va/content/francesco/en/speeches/2015/september/documents/papa-francesco_20150924_usa-us-congress.html.

177 Thomas D. Williams, "Pope Francis's praise of capitalism a surprise on US trip," *Crux* (September 21, 2016), https://cruxnow.com/commentary/2016/09/21/pope-franciss-praise-capitalism-surprise-us-trip/.

178 Collin Ruane, "Pope Francis: 'The Marxist ideology is wrong,'" *Atlanta Journal Constitution* (December 15, 2013), https://www.ajc.com/news/national/pope-francis-the-marxist-ideology-wrong/aNTHEz6PA621Kurl0ZHJWP/.

179 James M. Buchanan, What Should Economists Do? *Southern Economic Journal*, Vol. 30, No. 3 (January 1964), 213–222.

180 Kim Kelly, "What 'Capitalism' Is and How It Affects People," *Teen Vogue* (April 11, 2018), https://www.teenvogue.com/story/what-capitalism-is.

181 Emma Goldman, "Anarchy," *Emma Goldman: A Documentary History of the American Years, Volume One: Made for America 1890–1901*, ed. Candace Falk (Los Angeles, CA: University of California Press, 2008), 283.

182 Harry Kreisler, "Activism, Anarchism, and Power: Conversation with Nam Chomsky" (March 22, 2002), http://globetrotter.berkeley.edu/people2/Chomsky/chomsky-con2.html.

ENDNOTES

183 See, for example, Wilfred Carsel, "The Slaveholders' Indictment of Northern Wage Slavery," *The Journal of Southern History*, Vol. 6, No. 4 (November 1940), 504–520.

184 "I loathe hyperbole, but if a socialist government enforced the obligation to give away all your surplus to the poor, you would literally be a slave." Bryan Caplan, "Capitalism vs. Socialism: The Bruenig-Caplan Debate" (March 2018), https://www.econlib.org/archives/2018/03/capitalism_vs_s.html.

185 Karl Marx, *Capital*, Chapter XXV (1867), https://www.marxists.org/archive/marx/works/1867-c1/ch25.htm.

186 Robert Jensen, *Anti-Capitalism in Five Minutes Counter Punch* (April 30, 2007), https://www.counterpunch.org/2007/04/30/anti-capitalism-in-five-minutes/.

187 Robert A. Margo, "The Labor Force in the Nineteenth Century," *The Cambridge Economic History of the United States vol. II*, eds. Stanley L. Engerman and Robert E. Gallman (Cambridge: Cambridge University Press, 2000), 229-230.

188 Ethel B. Jones, "New Estimates of Hours of Work Per Week and Hourly Earnings, 1900–1957," *The Review of Economics and Statistics*, Vol. 45, No. 4 (November 1963), 375.

189 "Work and Workplace," *Gallup*, https://news.gallup.com/poll/1720/work-work-place.aspx.

190 Robert Jensen, *Anti-Capitalism in Five Minutes Counter Punch* (April 30, 2007), https://www.counterpunch.org/2007/04/30/anti-capitalism-in-five-minutes/.

191 François Bourguignon and Christian Morrison, "Inequality among World Citizens: 1820–1992," *The American Economic Review*, Vol. 92, No. 4. (September 2002) 733. Cited in Max Roser and Esteban Ortiz-Ospina, "Global Extreme Poverty," Our World in Data (March 27, 2017), https://ourworldindata.org/extreme-poverty.

192 "Nearly Half the World Lives on Less than $5.50 a Day," *The World Bank* (October 17, 2018), https://www.worldbank.org/en/news/press-release/2018/10/17/nearly-half-the-world-lives-on-less-than-550-a-day.

193 "Regional aggregation using 2011 PPP and $1.9/day poverty line," *The World Bank*, http://iresearch.worldbank.org/PovcalNet/povDuplicateWB.aspx Cited in Max Roser and Esteban Ortiz-Ospina, "Global Extreme Poverty" *Our World in Data* (March 27, 2017), https://ourworldindata.org/extreme-poverty.

194 Greg Mills, *Why Africa is Poor* (New York: Penguin Books, 2012), Kindle edition.

195 Paul Krugman, "Reckonings: Hearts and Heads" *The New York Times* (April 22, 2001), https://www.nytimes.com/2001/04/22/opinion/reckonings-hearts-and-heads.html.

196 Ludwig Von Mises, *Human Action: The Scholar's Edition* (Auburn, AL: Ludwig Von Mises Institute, 1998), 615.

197 *Summa Theologiae*, I–II, Q. 96, A. 2.

198 James C. Humes, *Churchill: The Prophetic Statesman* (Washington, D.C.: Regnery Books, 2012), 73.

199 Brianne Jacobs, "Yes, democratic socialism is compatible with Catholic social teaching," *America* (October 1, 2018), https://www.americamagazine.org/politics-society/2018/10/01/yes-democratic-socialism-compatible-catholic-social-teaching.

200 For an overview, see chapter seven of Barkley Rosser Jr. and Marina V. Rosser's *Comparative Economics in a Transforming World Economy* (2004).

201 See "2019 Index of Economic Freedom," https://www.heritage.org/index/ranking.

202 "Danish PM in US: Denmark is not socialist," *The Local* (November 1, 2015), https://www.thelocal.dk/20151101/danish-pm-in-us-denmark-is-not-socialist.

203 "None of the Nordic countries has a statutory minimum wage. Nor, with the exception of Finland, do they have a tradition of extending collective agreements to unorganized enterprises." Kristine Nergaard, "Social Democratic Capitalism," *The Oxford Handbook of Employment Relations*, eds. Adrian Wilkinson, Geoffrey Wood, Richard Deeg (Oxford: Oxford University Press, 2014),

204 "The 4.4 million or so Americans with Swedish origins are considerably richer than average Americans, as are other immigrant groups from Scandinavia. If Americans

with Swedish ancestry were to form their own country, their per capita GDP would be $56,900, more than $10,000 above the income of the average American. This is also far above Swedish GDP per capita, at $36,600. Swedes living in the USA are thus approximately 53 per cent more wealthy than Swedes (excluding immigrants) in their native country (OECD, 2009; US Census database)." Nima Sanandaji, "The surprising ingredients of Swedish success – free markets and social cohesion," *IEA Discussion Paper*, No. 41 (August 2012), https://iea.org.uk/wp-content/uploads/2016/07/Sweden percent20Paper.pdf.
205 "Voluntary health insurance in Europe: Country experience," *Observatory Studies Series*, No. 42. eds. A. Sagan and S. Thomson (2016), https://www.ncbi.nlm.nih.gov/books/NBK447719/.
206 Matt Phillips, "The High Price of a Free College Education in Sweden," *The Atlantic* (May 31, 2013), https://www.theatlantic.com/international/archive/2013/05/the-high-price-of-a-free-college-education-in-sweden/276428/.
207 "Only a small number of independent schools exist in Finland, and even they are all publicly financed. None is allowed to charge tuition fees. There are no private universities, either. This means that practically every person in Finland attends public school, whether for pre-K or a Ph.D." Anu Partanen, "What Americans Keep Ignoring About Finland's School Success," *The Atlantic* (December 29, 2011), https://www.theatlantic.com/national/archive/2011/12/what-americans-keep-ignoring-about-finlands-school-success/250564/. "Placing much more control in the hands of the government, the new law affects not only homeschoolers but all families in Sweden. The law now mandates a national curriculum and obliterates the notion of 'independent' (or private) schools and school choice." John Warwick Montgomery, "The Justification of Homeschooling Vis-à-vis the European Human Rights System," *Homeschooling in America and in Europe: A Litmus Test of Democracy*, ed. John Warwick Montgomery (Eugene, OR: Wipf and Stock, 2013), 80.
208 Marianne Frank Hansen and Marie Louise Schultz-Nielsen, "The fiscal impact of immigration to welfare states of the Scandinavian type," *Journal of Population Economics*, Vol. 30, Issue 3 (July 2017), 925–952.
209 Joe Weisenthal, "Obama: Swedish Model Would Be Impossible Here," *Business Insider* (February 11, 2009), https://www.businessinsider.com/obama-swedish-model-would-be-impossible-here-2009-2.
210 As of 2019, the countries with populations of more than 100 million include China, India, United States, Indonesia, Pakistan, Brazil, Nigeria, Bangladesh, Russia, Mexico, Japan, Ethiopia, and the Philippines. According to the Numbeo quality of life index, Japan scores a 180.5 and the U.S. scores a 179.2. The next closest is Mexico with a 123.48. The highest scoring country is Denmark with a 198.57. "Quality of Life Index for Country 2019," https://www.numbeo.com/quality-of-life/rankings_by_country.jsp?title=2019.
211 "Quality of Life Index 2019 Mid-Year," https://www.numbeo.com/quality-of-life/rankings.jsp.
212 Michael McCaughan, *The Battle of Venezuela* (New York: Seven Stories, 2005), 63.
213 Ibid., 65–66.
214 Adriana Bolívar, *Political Discourse as Dialogue: A Latin American Perspective* (New York: Routledge, 2018), electronic edition.
215 Mike Cole, *Critical Race Theory and Education: A Marxist Response* (New York: Palgrave Macmillan, 2009), 127.
216 Julie McCarthy, "Chavez Reaches Out with 'Bolivarian Missions,'" *NPR* (December 3, 2006), https://www.npr.org/templates/story/story.php?storyId=6572676.
217 Anthony Faiola, "In socialist Venezuela, a crisis of faith not in just their leader but their economic model," *The Washington Post* (February 11, 2019), https://www.washingtonpost.com/world/the_americas/in-socialist-venezuela-a-crisis-of-faith-

not-in-just-their-leader-but-their-economic-model/2019/02/11/ea67849e-2b33-11e9-906e-9d55b6451eb4_story.html.

218 "Full speed ahead," *The Economist* (October 29, 2010), https://www.economist.com/americas-view/2010/10/29/full-speed-ahead.

219 Emma Graham-Harrison, "Hunger eats away at Venezuela's soul as its people struggle to survive," *The Guardian* (August 26, 2017), https://www.theguardian.com/world/2017/aug/26/nicolas-maduro-donald-trump-venezuela-hunger.

220 James Suggett, "Chomsky praises Venezuela's revolution" *Green Left Weekly* (September 5, 2009), https://www.greenleft.org.au/content/chomsky-praises-venezuelas-revolution.

221 David Sirota, "Hugo Chavez's economic miracle," *Salon.com* (March 6, 2013), https://www.salon.com/2013/03/06/hugo_chavezs_economic_miracle/.

222 Jeffrey Webber, "Venezuela after Chávez," *Jacobin* (March 8, 2013), https://www.jacobinmag.com/2013/03/venezuela-after-chavez.

223 Mark Weisbrot, "Sorry, Venezuela Haters: This Economy Is Not the Greece of Latin America," *Common Dreams* (November 7, 2013), https://www.commondreams.org/views/2013/11/07/sorry-venezuela-haters-economy-not-greece-latin-america.

224 "Hugo Chavez declared the oil belonged 2 the ppl. He used the oil $ 2 eliminate 75 percent of extreme poverty, provide free health & education 4 all" (March 5, 2013). We have edited the tweet for readability. https://twitter.com/mmflint/status/309124649244057600?lang=en.

225 "Hated by the entrenched classes, Hugo Chavez will live forever in history. My friend, rest finally in a peace long earned. 2/2" (March 5, 2013), https://twitter.com/theoliverstone/status/309106639426949120.

226 Sam Jones, "Venezuela blackout: what caused it and what happens next?" *The Guardian* (March 13, 2019), https://www.theguardian.com/world/2019/mar/13/venezuela-blackout-what-caused-it-and-what-happens-next.

227 Anatoly Kurmanaev and John Otis, "Water Shortage Cripples Venezuela," *The Wall Street Journal* (April 3, 2016), https://www.wsj.com/articles/water-shortage-cripples-venezuela-1459717127. See also "Venezuelan water shortage deepens humanitarian crisis," *The Washington Post* (April 4, 2019), https://www.washingtonpost.com/world/the_americas/why-are-you-crying-mami-in-venezuela-the-search-for-water-is-a-daily-struggle/2019/04/04/39972ce4-5547-11e9-814f-e2f46684196e_story.html.

228 "Venezuela: New regime effectively amounts to forced labour," *Amnesty International* (July 28, 2016), https://www.amnesty.org/en/latest/news/2016/07/venezuela-new-regime-effectively-amounts-to-forced-labour/.

229 Vivian Sequera, "Venezuelans report big weight losses in 2017 as hunger hits," *Reuters* (February 21, 2018), https://www.reuters.com/article/us-venezuela-food/venezuelans-report-big-weight-losses-in-2017-as-hunger-hits-idUSKCN1G52HA.

230 Jenny García, Gerardo Correa, and Brenda Rousset, "Trends in infant mortality in Venezuela between 1985 and 2016: a systematic analysis of demographic data," *The Lancet* Vol. 7, Issue 3, (March 1, 2019), https://www.thelancet.com/journals/langlo/article/PIIS2214-109X(18)30479-0/fulltext.

231 Megan Specia, "Five Things You Need to Know to Understand Venezuela's Crisis," *The New York Times* (May 3, 2019), https://www.nytimes.com/2019/05/03/world/americas/venezuela-crisis-facts.html.

232 Renzo Pipoli, "Maduro raises minimum wage in Venezuela to $6 per month," *United Press International* (January 15, 2019), https://www.upi.com/Top_News/World-News/2019/01/15/Maduro-raises-minimum-wage-in-Venezuela-to-6-per-month/9171547575404/.

233 Fabiola Zerpa, "In Venezuela, a Haircut Costs 5 Bananas and 2 Eggs," *Bloomberg* (May 4, 2018), https://www.bloomberg.com/news/articles/2018-05-04/in-caracus-venezuela-a-haircut-costs-five-bananas-and-two-eggs.

234 "The United Nations says more than 4 million refugees and migrants have left the

country, which is suffering from political chaos, food shortages and hyperinflation. The U.N. has called this exodus the 'largest in the recent history of Latin America and the Caribbean.'" Merritt Kennedy, "U.N. Says More Than 4 Million People Have Left Venezuela," *NPR* (June 7, 2019), https://www.npr.org/2019/06/07/730687807/u-n-says-more-than-4-million-people-have-left-venezuela.

235 Daniel Di Martino, "Venezuela was my home, and socialism destroyed it. Slowly, it will destroy America, too," *USA Today* (February 15, 2019), https://www.usatoday.com/story/opinion/voices/2019/02/15/donald-trump-venezuela-socialism-bernie-sanders-ilhan-omar-column/2861461002/.

236 Fyodor Dostoyevsky, *The Brothers Karamazov* (New York: Dover, 2005), 56.

237 "Tradinista Manifesto," https://tradinista.tumblr.com/manifesto.

238 "Ortega supporters try to infiltrate parishes. Security forces surround churches during Mass. Priests suffer harassment and death threats. Police ring the Jesuit university when students dare to wave Nicaraguan flags and chant anti-government slogans." Mary Beth Sheridan, "Spies, harassment, death threats: The Catholic Church in Nicaragua says it's being targeted by the government." *The Washington Post* (July 23, 2019), https://www.washingtonpost.com/world/the_americas/spies-harassment-death-threats-the-catholic-church-in-nicaragua-says-its-being-targeted-by-the-government/2019/07/23/2881f814-a3ec-11e9-a767-d7ab84aef3e9_story.html.

239 Matthew Schmitz, "I Think I'm Not a Contra," *First Things* (September 29, 2016), https://www.firstthings.com/blogs/firstthoughts/2016/09/i-think-im-not-a-contra.

240 "Employment by industry, 1910 and 2015," Bureau of Labor Statistics (March 3, 2016), https://www.bls.gov/opub/ted/2016/employment-by-industry-1910-and-2015.htm.

241 Jose Mena, "The Catholic turn to socialism is something to celebrate," *Catholic Herald* (May 30, 2019), https://catholicherald.co.uk/commentandblogs/2019/05/30/the-catholic-turn-to-socialism-is-something-to-celebrate/.

242 Matthew Shadle, "Tradinistas: A New Catholic Socialism?, Part 2," *Political Theology Network* (October 9, 2016), https://politicaltheology.com/tradinistas-a-new-catholic-socialism-part-2-matthew-shadle/.

243 Ronald Reagan, "Socialism," *Stories in His Own Hand: The Everyday Wisdom of Ronald Reagan*, eds. Kiron K. Skinner, Annelise Anderson, and Martin Anderson (New York: The Free Press, 2001), 91. This quote comes from a letter Reagan wrote in 1976 about a young conservative named Brad Linaweaver's interaction with a woman who was defending socialism. Brad said that government should guarantee people not just food and medicine but also a yacht. When his critic said that people like him were what kept socialism from working, he deftly replied, "How many are there like me?" That's why the original quote ends by saying, "They don't understand that we dream—yes, even of sometime owning a yacht."

244 *Instruction on Certain Aspects of the "Theology of Liberation,"* 15.

245 "Across these experiments, the main variable that we find that consistently explains this differential pattern of giving and helping and generosity among the upper and lower class is feelings of sensitivity and care for the welfare of other people and, essentially, the emotion that we call compassion. So it's really compassionate feelings that exist among the lower class that's seen to provoke these higher levels of altruism and generosity toward other people." "Study: Poor Are More Charitable than the Wealthy," *National Public Radio* (August 8, 2010), https://www.npr.org/templates/story/story.php?storyId=129068241.

246 Norman Lamm, *The Shema: Spirituality and Law in Judaism* (Philadelphia: The Jewish Publication Society, 2000), 142.

247 "Take the most advanced case: Mondragon. It's worker owned, it's not worker managed, although the management does come from the workforce often, but it's in a market system and they still exploit workers in South America, and they do things that are harmful to the society as a whole and they have no choice. If you're in a

system where you must make profit in order to survive, you're compelled to ignore negative externalities, effects on others." Laura Flanders, "Talking with Chomsky," *Counterpunch* (April 30, 2012), https://www.counterpunch.org/2012/04/30/talking-with-chomsky/.

248 Edward Feser, "Hayek's Tragic Capitalism," *The Claremont Review of Books* (Spring 2019), 88.

249 "Do We Agree? A Debate Between G. K. Chesterton And Bernard Shaw," http://www.gkc.org.uk/gkc/books/debate.txt.

250 Hilaire Belloc, Economics for Helen (London: J.W. Arrowsmith, 1924), 125. Cited in Thomas Woods, *The Church and the Market* (Lanham, MD: Lexington Books, 2015). Kindle edition.

251 Russell Sparkes "Chesterton as Economist," *The Hounds of Distributism* ed. Richard Aleman (Charlotte, NC: The American Chesterton Society, 2015), kindle edition.

252 David W. Cooney. *Distributism Basics: An Explanation* (Self Published, 2016). Kindle edition.

253 Ibid.

254 Ibid.

255 *Sollicitudo Rei Socialis*, 41.

256 *Centesimus Annus*, 43.

257 David W. Cooney, *Distributism Basics: An Explanation* (Self Published, 2016). Kindle edition.

258 Ibid.

259 John Medaille, "A Distributist Banking System," *The Hound of Distributism* ed. Richard Aleman (Charlotte, NC: The American Chesterton Society, 2015), kindle edition.

260 *Quadragesimo Anno,* 42.

261 *The Hounds of Distributism* ed. Richard Aleman (Charlotte, NC: The American Chesterton Society, 2015).

262 David Deavel, "What's Wrong with Distributism?" *Intercollegiate Studies Institute* (August 5, 2013).

263 Derek Thompson, "How America Spends Money: 100 Years in the Life of the Family Budget," *The Atlantic* (April 5, 2012), https://www.theatlantic.com/business/archive/2012/04/how-america-spends-money-100-years-in-the-life-of-the-family-budget/255475/.

264 Chad Otar, "What Percentage Of Small Businesses Fail—And How Can You Avoid Being One Of Them?," *Forbes* (October 25, 2018), https://www.forbes.com/sites/forbesfinancecouncil/2018/10/25/what-percentage-of-small-businesses-fail-and-how-can-you-avoid-being-one-of-them/#2d444c4143b5.

265 "The Top 20 Reasons Startups Fail," CB Insights Research Briefs (November 6, 2019), https://www.cbinsights.com/research/startup-failure-reasons-top/.

266 Thomas Woods, *The Church and the Market* (Lanham, MD: Lexington Books, 2015). Kindle edition.

267 "Education, Skills, and Technical Change: Implications for Future U.S. GDP Growth," (2019), https://www.nber.org/books/hult-12.

ABOUT THE AUTHORS

After his conversion to the Catholic faith, **Trent Horn** earned master's degrees in the fields of theology, philosophy, and bioethics. He serves as a staff apologist for Catholic Answers, where he specializes in teaching Catholics to graciously and persuasively engage those who disagree with them. Trent models that approach each week on the radio program *Catholic Answers Live* and on his own podcast, *The Counsel of Trent*. He has also been invited to debate at UC Berkeley, UC Santa Barbara, and Stanford University. Trent is an adjunct professor of apologetics at Holy Apostles College, has written for *The National Catholic Bioethics Quarterly*, and is the author of nine books, including *Answering Atheism*, *The Case for Catholicism*, and *Why We're Catholic: Our Reasons for Faith, Hope, and Love*.

Catherine Ruth Pakaluk, Ph.D, is assistant professor at the Busch School of Business at The Catholic University of America. She specializes in the economics of education and religion, family studies and demography, Catholic social thought, and political economy. Pakaluk earned her doctorate at Harvard University in 2010 where she studied under 2016 Nobel-laureate Oliver Hart. She has authored and co-authored highly cited articles in journals including *Economic Inquiry*, *Journal of Markets and Morality*, *Demography*, and the *Journal of the National Cancer Institute*. Pakaluk is a widely admired writer and sought-after speaker on matters of culture, gender, social science, the vocation of women, and the work of Edith Stein. She lives in Maryland with her husband, philosopher Michael Pakaluk, and eight children.